11

Boris Godunov

Modest Mussorgsky

Opera Guide Series Editor: Nicholas John

Published in association with English National Opera and The Royal Opera

John Calder · London
Riverrun Press · New York

First published in Great Britain, 1982, by
John Calder (Publishers) Ltd, 18 Brewer Street,
London W1R 4AS

and

First Published in U.S.A., 1982, by
Riverrun Press Inc.,
175 Fifth Avenue,
New York, NY 10010

BRITISH LIBRARY CATALOGUING DATA

Mussorgsky, Modest
  Boris Godunov — (English National Opera guides: 11)
  1. Mussorgsky, Modest. Boris Godunov
  2. Operas — Librettos
  I. Title   II. John, Nicholas   III. Series
  782.1'092'4   ML410.M9
ISBN 0-7145-3922-8

SUBSIDISED BY THE
Arts Council
OF GREAT BRITAIN

John Calder (Publishers) Ltd, English National Opera and The
Royal Opera House, Covent Garden Ltd receive financial assis-
tance from the Arts Council of Great Britain. English National
Opera also receives financial assistance from the Greater London
Council.

Typeset in Plantin by Margaret Spooner Typesetting

Printed and bound in Great Britain by Collins, Glasgow.

Opera
Guide

Boris
Godunov
Mussorgsky

Fyodor Chaliapin as Boris. The unforgettable experience of Chaliapin's performance has been many times described: Victor Gollancz in 'Journey Towards Music' likens the voice 'to Casals' cello — above everything . . . some unanalysable residue in his voice and way of singing made him unique'. (Stuart-Liff Collection)

Preface

This series, published under the auspices of English National Opera and The Royal Opera, aims to prepare audiences to enjoy and evaluate opera performances. Each book contains the complete text, set out in the original language together with a current performing translation. The accompanying essays have been commissioned as general introductions to aspects of interest in each work. As many illustrations and musical examples as possible have been included because the sound and spectacle of opera are clearly central to any sympathetic appreciation of it. We hope that, as ideal companions to the opera should be, they are well-informed, witty and attractive.

Nicholas John
Series Editor

Contents

List of Illustrations

Looking into 'Boris Godunov'

Robert W. Oldani

On January 27, 1874 (Old Style), Modest Mussorgsky's opera *Boris Godunov* received its first performance at the Maryinsky Theatre in St Petersburg. Several of the most popular singers of the Maryinsky troupe took part, including Ivan Melnikov as Boris, Yulia Platonova as Marina, and Osip Petrov as Varlaam. The conductor was Eduard Napravnik, a Czech musician and composer who altogether would spend more than forty years as the chief conductor of the Maryinsky. The sets were probably those created more than three years earlier for the première of Alexander Pushkin's *Boris Godunov*, the play from which Mussorgsky had derived his libretto.

Even then, the opera was presented in a form notably different from the form in which the composer finally had left it; Napravnik omitted, for instance, the entire scene in Pimen's cell. Thus, from the beginning, one is confronted with the central irony concerning *Boris Godunov*: rarely has it been performed as the composer wrote it. Much of the blame, of course, rests with Nikolay Rimsky-Korsakov, whose revision of the opera has held the stage now for three-quarters of a century, but some must rest with Mussorgsky himself, who completed two distinct versions. Additional redactions by other musicians, including Dimitry Shostakovich, further complicate the matter. The producer of *Boris Godunov* thus faces many alternatives, and the problem is only partly solved by confining oneself to 'what Mussorgsky wrote'. The purpose of this essay, then, is to place the opera in the context of its time, to sketch the history of its composition and first performance, and to acquaint the reader with some of the facts of the so-called '*Boris* problem'.

For more than a century before Mussorgsky's birth, both foreign and native musicians had composed opera in Russia. In the eighteenth century the genre thrived primarily at the Imperial court, and foreign works, largely by Italian composers, were both more numerous and more popular than native ones. Works based on heroic and patriotic subjects became popular after Napoleon's defeat in 1812, and the crowning achievement among such works, performed for the first time in 1836, is Mikhail Glinka's *Life for the Tsar*, based on the tale of a peasant – Ivan Susanin – who sacrifices his life to save Tsar Mikhail, founder of the Romanov dynasty. Glinka's opera impressed the emperor Nicholas I favourably: in Gerald Abraham's words, to see *A Life for the Tsar* became almost 'a patriotic duty', and Glinka 'found himself recognized as "the first composer in Russia" '.

First composer or not, Glinka discovered in the 1840s that his countrymen had not entirely lost their taste for Italian opera. His second opera, *Ruslan and Lyudmila*, although musically more advanced than *A Life for the Tsar*, was received with far less excitement. According to the composer's memoirs, 'the applause [at the première in November 1842] was really not very enthusiastic and there was some active hissing . . .'. By contrast, when the Italian tenor Giovanni Battista Rubini visited St Petersburg in 1843, giving several concerts during Lent, he provoked great enthusiasm. The critic for the newspaper *Northern Bee* wrote:

> What is there to say about Rubini? . . . Whether he sang better at some time we do not know, but we believe that with merely a human throat *it is impossible to sing better!* . . . This is not a voice, but some pure stream of harmony falling from heaven and penetrating the heart! To speak of art? It was taken up to the highest degree, to the *ne plus ultra!*

Rubini's success led to the rebirth of Italian opera in St Petersburg. Each year from 1843 until 1885 the Director of the Imperial Theatres engaged foreign singers to perform a season of opera in Italian in the capital. Although another company, composed primarily of native singers, performed foreign and native works in Russian throughout the period as well, in the 1840s and 1850s they sang in the shadow of the Italians.

In the 1860s, however, opportunity presented itself to Russian singers and composers. For several reasons, the popularity of opera in Italian declined, and opera in Russian, by both Russian and foreign composers, began to enjoy greater success than it ever had before. For example, Verdi's *Forza del Destino*, commissioned by the Imperial Theatres and given its first performance by the Italian troupe in 1862, was lampooned by one Russian writer as yet another 'tragedy in blood' by the cynical composer of such masterpieces as *Suicide When the Horn Sounds, Assassination in America*, and *The Tubercular Tart*; another critic begged to hear Glinka's music as an antidote to Verdi's. As though in answer to this prayer, the Maryinsky company successfully revived *Ruslan and Lyudmila* in 1864. Furthermore, Alexander Serov's *Judith* (1863), based on the Apocryphal story of Judith and Holofernes, and *Rogneda* (1865), based on a tale of Kievan Russia, both enjoyed great and immediate popularity.

Mussorgsky made his first serious attempts to compose an opera in these auspicious years. He began *Salammbô*, based on Gustave Flaubert's tale of ancient Carthage, less than six months after the successful première of *Judith*, probably while under that work's spell. Although he worked on the score intermittently for three years, he finished just six numbers, about ninety minutes of music, some of which ultimately found its way into *Boris Godunov*. After another false start, an almost word-for-word setting of Nikolay Gogol's prose comedy *The Marriage*, he finally found in a suggestion by his friend Vladimir Nikolsky the subject for which he had been searching — Pushkin's *Boris Godunov*. But by that time, October 1868, the years of decline at the Italian opera were nearly over. Less than three months after Mussorgsky had written the first bars of *Boris Godunov*, Adelina Patti made her triumphant debut in St Petersburg. She became so popular that she was re-engaged each year until 1877. And during the nine years in which Patti and the Italian repertory so suited to her talents reigned over opera in St Petersburg, *Boris Godunov* was composed, rejected for production, revised, and given its première.

*

Like so many other young Russians of his day, Mussorgsky was fascinated by his country's past. In 1858, upon visiting Moscow, he had been awestruck by the Kremlin and St Basil's Cathedral, describing them as 'sacred antiquity'. Later, he enthusiastically read the works of such historians of his native land as Nikolay Karamzin and Sergey Soloviev, and he once confessed to his friend Vladimir Stasov: 'History is my nocturnal mate — I absorb it and more than enjoy it, despite my weariness and my dismal mornings at the office'.

But in the early 1860s, Pushkin's *Boris Godunov* would have been an impractical choice of subject for any composer. Although the play had been written in 1825, published in 1831, and reprinted several times after the poet's death in 1837, the tsarist censor did not approve it for performance on stage until 1866. It finally received its first performance in September 1870. Despite the work's literary excellence, it seems to have been unsuccessful in the theatre; only the sets were praised uniformly for their beauty and historical accuracy. According to one theatre historian 'The performance was facile, even, and conscientious, but no one was remarkably distinguished ... The highly poetic scene by the fountain passed by limply. The comedy with couplets *The Claws of St Petersburg* by Messrs Khudyakov and Zhulev had an incomparably greater success'.

Boris Christoff, the Bulgarian bass who first sang Boris at Covent Garden in 1949, in the coronation scene.

In the autumn of 1868, midway between the censor's approval of the play and its performance, Mussorgsky began his opera. Work progressed rapidly, and the entire project – from compilation of the libretto to orchestration – was completed by December of 1869. This initial version of the opera contains seven scenes grouped in four parts, as follows: Part One: Courtyard of the Novodievichy Monastery and Coronation; Part Two: Pimen's Cell and An Inn on the Lithuanian Frontier; Part Three: The Tsar's Apartments in the Kremlin; Part Four: The Square before St Basil's Cathedral and Boris's Death. There is no Polish Act and no scene in Kromy Forest in the initial version.

When Mussorgsky completed his score, no opera was produced at the Maryinsky Theatre without first being examined by both a literary and a music committee, whose task was to prevent a work with either a poor libretto or bad music from reaching the stage. In addition, usually before reaching these committees, an opera had to pass through the state censorship, where its libretto faced close scrutiny. Neither the composer's prestige at home nor his European fame exempted his work from these examinations. Anton Rubinstein, for example, enjoyed far greater prestige than Mussorgsky in the 'sixties and 'seventies, but his opera *The Demon* passed through the same trials as *Boris Godunov*. The music committee accepted *The Demon* in September of 1871, but the censorship at first refused to permit the performance of a work in which an evil spirit was portrayed, and the première of Rubinstein's work was delayed for more than three years.

Mussorgsky submitted his opera in 1870. Although it unquestionably faced problems of censorship — a specific rule against showing any Tsar on stage in opera, vaguer prohibitions against so-called harmful attitudes and anti-governmental tendencies — we have good reason to suppose that it received the censor's approval, but the Maryinsky's music committee rejected it by a vote of six to one. According to the memoirs of Rimsky-Korsakov, written some thirty-five years after the event, the reasons for this rejection were 'the freshness and originality of the music' and the lack of an important female role.[1]

Whatever the reasons for rejection, Mussorgsky enthusiastically began to

[1] Perhaps one should not be too surprised at the rejection of the first completed opera by an unproven composer on the subject of a play which had just failed.

revise the work at once. Is it likely that he would have undertaken so readily the revision of what to him was a satisfactorily completed work without some assurance that the changes would lead to a performance? Indeed, we find an indication of just such an assurance in the memoirs of Lyudmila Shestakova, Glinka's sister. She describes a luncheon she attended on the day *Boris* was rejected. Having asked theatre officials who were present whether the opera had been accepted, she received the reply: 'No, it is impossible for an opera without a female element! Undoubtedly, Mussorgsky has great talent; let him add another scene, then *Boris* would be accepted'.

The history of the revision is quite complex. At first Mussorgsky appears to have intended only to add the Polish scenes, thereby providing the missing 'female element', but by mid-summer of 1871 he had decided on a more extensive revision.[1] In the end, he transferred five of the seven scenes of the initial version (Novodievichy, Coronation, Cell, Inn, Death) – even these with some modifications – directly to the revision. He recomposed a sixth, the scene in the tsar's apartments. He omitted the seventh, the St Basil scene, but stitched a few of its pages (the Simpleton and the children, and his lament) into an entirely new scene, the scene of anarchy in Kromy Forest; and, of course, he added the two Polish scenes. The revision thus contains nine scenes, which the composer finally grouped into a prologue and four acts. Interestingly enough, the idea of placing the newly composed scene near Kromy at the end of the opera, after the death of Boris, was apparently not Mussorgsky's. According to Stasov, 'this so very important change was suggested to the composer by his friend Vladimir Nikolsky [who the reader will recall had sent Mussorgsky to Pushkin's *Boris* in the first place]. Mussorgsky was ecstatic, and in a few days he had redesigned and adjusted this conclusion'.[2]

The Maryinsky Theatre's music committee examined the revision in the spring of 1872, about six weeks before Mussorgsky completed the orchestration. Writers on the composer usually maintain that the work was rejected a second time at this second examination, but the evidence for this is not convincing. The result of the second examination was probably, on the contrary, provisional acceptance. After all, Mussorgsky was able to bring the committee a completed piano-vocal score answering their previous objections, approval of the censor, and authorization from the tsar himself. He had *not* completed the orchestral score, and so the committee may have been reluctant to guarantee the production of the work in the coming season (1872–73). Furthermore, since they intended to mount both the initial production of Rimsky-Korsakov's *Maid of Pskov* and a revival of Wagner's *Lohengrin* in 1872–73, the committee may have been reluctant to commit themselves to *Boris*, a third major undertaking. Rather, they

[1] According to Vladimir Stasov, Mussorgsky had prepared 'splendid materials' for the scene by the fountain long before the opera's rejection. 'God knows,' Stasov writes, 'why he abandoned them in the first place.'

[2] Although Mussorgsky may have followed his friends' advice concerning his works more often than most great composers, he was quite capable of resisting when he thought they were wrong. Again, according to Stasov, 'Originally, the opera *Boris Godunov* was to consist of only four acts and was almost completely devoid of a female element. All Mussorgsky's closest friends (including me), who rapturously loved the miracles of drama and folk-truth with which these four acts were filled, nevertheless told him every minute that the opera was not complete, that many essential things were missing in it, and that despite its great beauties, the work could seem at times incomplete. Mussorgsky, like any genuine artist, always persistently defended his work, the fruit of reflections and inspirations. For a long time he did not agree with us and finally yielded to our power only when in the fall of 1870 (sic) the Theatre Directorate refused to mount *Boris* on stage on the grounds that there was a prevalence of choruses and ensembles and a too-sensible absence of scenes for soloists.'

probably told Mussorgsky that the revision made the opera acceptable and that they would produce it at some unspecified future date.

As things turned out, once the productions of *The Maid of Pskov* and *Lohengrin* were past, the Maryinsky was able to produce three scenes from *Boris*, perhaps partly as a gesture of good faith and partly as a result of the interest several artists of the troupe took in the work. On February 5, 1873, the scene at the inn and the two Polish scenes were staged at the *bénéfice* of Gennady Kondratiev, the theatre's chief director. Reviews of this performance were generally favourable; public enthusiasm was unusually high.

In the following season, on January 27, 1874, *Boris Godunov* finally received its first full performance, but several passages appearing in the published piano-vocal score were omitted. Although the largest cut by far was the entire scene in Pimen's cell, parts of other scenes were omitted too, for example, in Act Two the 'Song of the Parrot' and some two dozen particularly dissonant measures involving the chiming clock. Contrary to popular belief, the tsarist censor does not seem to have demanded these omissions. Rather, the blame lies primarily with the conductor Napravnik, who frequently cut passages that he thought theatrically ineffective, no matter who the composer. Mussorgsky, of course, chose to accept these cuts rather than sacrifice the performance. Prudence in matters concerning the censorship may have given him a rationalization that the loss of the Cell scene perhaps was for the best, but the censor's direct effect was minimal.

Although the public responded enthusiastically to the opera, most critics received it with hostility. For example, Alexander Famintsyn, who had been a professor at the St Petersburg Conservatory, excoriated Mussorgsky for his

George London was the first non-Russian to sing Boris at the Bolshoi in 1960. (Met. Archives)

Italo Tajo as Boris (Stuart-Liff Collection)

unresolved discords, parallel fifths, chaotically mixed tonalities, cross-relations, excessive use of pedal point, and nonsensical chord progressions. He acknowledged that the work had achieved a great success and, finding its success difficult to reconcile with the obvious weaknesses that he had pointed out, speculated that the opera's subject and the splendour of its staging were responsible for its popularity. Despite such criticism, the opera remained popular with the public. In the seasons of 1873–74 and 1874–75, twelve performances were given before full or nearly full houses. After a year's absence from the repertory, *Boris Godunov* was revived in October of 1876 (with the further omission of the Kromy Forest scene), and it received an additional fourteen performances, before enthusiastic if not always full houses, prior to its removal — for which no official reasons were given — from the repertory in November of 1882.

*

Mussorgsky has bequeathed producers difficult choices: whether to perform the initial *Boris*, completed in 1869, the revision, published in 1874, or a combination of the two. Some simply choose one or the other of Mussorgsky's versions and stick to it; others choose the revision but insert into it, say, the St Basil scene and perhaps Pimen's narrative about the murder of the Tsarevich Dimitry; still others choose the initial version but substitute the revised second act and add, for example, the hostess's 'Song of the Duck'. The problems perhaps admit of no solution satisfactory to all.

Producers who consider redactions of the opera by other musicians are faced with still more choices. Rimsky-Korsakov first published his version of *Boris* in 1896, making many changes and taking lengthy cuts. Ten years later, he restored some of these cuts, and then he expanded the Coronation scene for Diaghilev's production in Paris. In 1926 Mikhail Ippolitov-Ivanov orchestrated the St Basil scene in Rimsky's manner, so that this additional 'people's scene' could be included in Soviet performances using Rimsky's score. In 1940, Shostakovich completed an orchestration of *Boris Godunov* working directly from the piano-vocal score edited by the Soviet musicologist Pavel Lamm – itself a conflation of Mussorgsky's initial and revised versions. Shostakovich's score thus perpetuates Lamm's conflation, and in addition, in the initial version of the scene in the tsar's quarters, Shostakovich recommends a further conflation unforeseen by Mussorgsky, Rimsky, Ippolitov, or Lamm! Clearly, it is easy to lose sight of Mussorgsky's achievement amidst all these 'versions'.

But what then *is* Mussorgsky's achievement? One could speak of recurring themes, tonal-dramatic associations, key relationships, declamatory and lyric writing, Western models, empiricism, and the composer's aspiration to reproduce 'human speech in all its finest shades', and these would each tell part of the story. But the appeal of *Boris Godunov* to our emotions transcends its orchestral dress. In the last scene, for instance, whether in the orchestration of Mussorgsky or Shostakovich[1], we perceive a desolation unsurpassed in opera before *Wozzeck*. The theatrical force of *Boris* ensures its place, in any version, in the world's opera houses. In Russia, it ranks second only to those of Glinka. In the West, no other Russian opera, not even Tchaikovsky's *Evgeny Onegin*, has come nearer the status of a repertory piece. Stasov's prophecy that Mussorgsky's operas would 'go further afield than the rest' has been fulfilled in *Boris Godunov*, and yet in 1868 no one, least of all Mussorgsky, foresaw such a result. Shortly before beginning work on *Boris*, Mussorgsky complained to a friend: 'And why is everything only a preparation – it's about time to do something! My trifling little pieces were preparations, *The Marriage* is a preparation – whenever will something finally be ready?' With the completion of *Boris Godunov*, he had the answer to his question.

[1] Rimsky-Korsakov, of course, inverted the order of the scenes of Act IV, so that his version ends not with the Simpleton's lament, but with Boris's death.

Mikhail Mikhailov as Pimen

Leonid Savransky as Boris

Helen Sadoven as Marina

Mark Reizen as Boris

13

A Comparison of Mussorgsky's Versions of 'Boris'

Initial Version [completed December 1869]	Revised Version [published January 1874]
Part I, Scene 1: Courtyard of the Novodievichy Monastery.	Prologue, Scene 1: Courtyard of the Novodievichy Monastery.

A. Introduction.	A. Introduction.
B. Policeman's orders.	B. Policeman's orders.
C. People's chorus of supplication.	C. People's chorus of supplication.
D. Policeman's return, further orders.	D. Policeman's return, further orders.
E. Second chorus of supplication.	E. Second chorus of supplication.
F. Schelkalov's address to the people.	F. Shchelkalov's address to the people.
G. Chorus of pilgrims.	G. Chorus of pilgrims.
H. Final scene between the people and the policeman.	—

Part I, Scene 2: Coronation	Prologue, Scene 2: Coronation (5 bars shorter).

Part II, Scene 1: Cell in the Chudov Monastery.	Act I, Scene 1: Cell in the Chudov Monastery.

A. Pimen's monologue.	A. Pimen's monologue.
—	B/a. First chorus of monks behind the scene;
B. Grigory's awakening.	b. Grigory's awakening.
—	C/a. Second chorus of monks behind the scene;
C. Grigory's account of his dream and subsequent dialogue with Pimen.	b. Grigory's account of his dream and subsequent dialogue with Pimen.
D. Pimen's story of the tsars.	D. Pimen's story of the tsars.
E/a. Pimen's narrative of the murder of Dimitry;	—
b. Grigory's question.	E. Grigory's question.
F. Chorus of monks behind the scene and conclusion.	F. Third chorus of monks behind the scene and conclusion.

Part II, Scene 2: Inn on the Lithuanian Frontier.	Act I, Scene 2: Inn on the Lithuanian Frontier.

A. Introduction.	A/a. Introduction.
—	b. Hostess's "Song of the Duck".
B. Arrival of Grigory, Varlaam, and Missail.	B. Arrival of Grigory, Varlaam, and Missail.
C. Varlaam's first song ("Ballad of Kazan").	C. Varlaam's first song ("Ballad of Kazan").
D. Varlaam's second song and Grigory's conversation with the hostess.	D. Varlaam's second song and Grigory's conversation with the hostess.
E. Arrival of the policemen.	E. Arrival of the policemen.
F. The reading of the warrant and conclusion.	F. The reading of the warrant and conclusion.

Part III: The Tsar's Quarters in the Kremlin.			Act II: The Tsar's Quarters in the Kremlin.	
A.	Xenia's lament; Feodor sings at his map.		A/a.	Xenia's lament; Feodor silent at the map.
—			b.	The children with the chiming clock.
B.	Nurse's attempt to comfort Xenia.		B/a.	Nurse's attempt to comfort Xenia.
—			b.	Song of the Gnat.
—			c.	Handclapping Game.
C.	Boris's entry; he comforts Xenia.		C.	Boris's entry; he comforts Xenia.
D.	Boris and Feodor at the map.		D.	Boris and Feodor at the map.
E.	Boris's monologue.		E.	Boris's monologue.
—			F/a.	Tumult of nurses behind the scene.
F.	Boyar's denunciation of Shuisky.		b.	Boyar's denunciation of Shuisky.
			c.	Feodor's "Song of the Parrot".
G.	Boris's scene with Shuisky.		G.	Boris's scene with Shuisky.
H.	Shuisky's description of Dimitry's body.		H.	Shuisky's description of Dimitry's body.
I.	Boris's hallucination.		I.	Boris's hallucination, with the chiming clock.

—		Act III, Scene 1: Marina's Boudoir.	
—		Act III, Scene 2: Garden by the Fountain.	

Part IV, Scene 1: Square before St Basil's Cathedral.		—	

Part IV, Scene 2: Granovitaya Palace (Death of Boris).			Act IV, Scene 1: Granovitaya Palace (Death of Boris).	
A/a.	Introduction.		A.	Introduction.
b.	Shchelkalov's reading of the ukase.		—	
B.	Chorus of boyars.		B.	Chorus of boyars.
C.	Shuisky's arrival and narration.		C.	Shuisky's arrival and narration (28 bars shorter).
D.	Entry of Boris.		D.	Entry of Boris.
E.	Pimen's narrative.		E.	Pimen's narrative (6 bars shorter).
F.	Farewell and death of Boris.		F.	Farewell (13 bars shorter) and death of Boris.

—	Act IV, Scene 2: A Forest Glade near Kromy. [Two of this scene's seven sections are transferred from the otherwise discarded St Basil's scene: the episode of the fool with the boys and the fool's concluding lament.]

This table originally appeared as the appendix to an article published in the *Liberal Arts Review*, and it has been reprinted in my contribution to the book *Musorgsky: In Memoriam, 1881–1981*. I wish to thank the editors of both these publications for permission to reproduce it in this monograph.

Sources consulted in this essay include Abraham *On Russian Music* (London, 1939), Glinka *Memoirs* (trans. R.B. Mudge; Norman, Oklahoma 1963), N. Rimsky-Korsakov *My Musical Life* (trans. J. Joffe; New York 1942), R. Newmarch *The Russian Opera* (London, 1914), and my own articles: 'Mussorgsky's *Boris Godunov* and the Russian Imperial Theatres' (Liberal Arts Review No. 7, Spring 1979) and '*Boris Godunov* and the Censor' (Nineteenth-Century Music 2; March, 1979). *R.W. Oldani*

The Historical Background

Nicholas John

Boris Godunov was born in 1550, during the reign of Tsar Ivan IV, known as 'The Terrible'. The Godunov family was not of Boyar lineage but descended from one of the first Tartar princes to swear allegiance to the Grand Princes of Moscow. Boris became Ivan's most trusted counsellor after the pogroms carried out against the Boyars. In 1580 Ivan took a seventh wife. At the same ceremony he married his younger son, Fyodor, to Boris Godunov's sister. The double wedding was both the source of the Godunovs' ascendancy and of their nemesis. Dimitry, whose name was to haunt Boris's life, was the child of the Tsar's marriage (a marriage that was never recognised by the Church), while Fyodor's marriage gave Boris equal status with the representatives of the Shuisky and Romanov families who already had legitimate claims to the throne.

Fyodor became Tsar in 1584 and Boris gained increasing control of the government in his name.

In 1591, Dimitry met a violent death in Uglich near Moscow. Many, led by his mother's family and the Godunovs' enemies, suspected that Boris had ordered the child's murder, to assure his path to the throne. Boris made every effort to clear his reputation by appointing a hostile boyar, Shuisky, to conduct the official enquiry. He reported that Dimitry had fallen on his knife during an epileptic fit.

Seven years later, Fyodor, the last of the Rurik dynasty which had ruled for twenty-one generations, died naming his wife as his heir. She refused to rule as Tsaritsa and became a nun; then she begged her brother to accept the crown instead. Boris retired to a monastery for prayer and the guidance of God.

After miracle-working icons had been brought to the monastery, Boris yielded to the entreaties of his supporters. His coronation was celebrated in 1598 with an exceptional magnificence that astounded all observers — the more to impress on them his right to the throne. In the following year, a monk formerly in the service of the Romanovs, Grigory Otrepyev, fled to Lithuania and claimed to be Dimitry. He was excommunicated by the Orthodox Church.

In 1601, a terrible famine caused by extraordinary climatic conditions was interpreted as a sign of God's curse on Boris. 500,000 died in Moscow alone. The Romanovs spread rumours that Dimitry had somehow survived 'the murder'.

Catholic Poland was inevitably opposed to Orthodox Russia and Grigory found many supporters among the Poles who were willing to support his claims, whether or not they believed them. He asked to marry Marina Mniszek, daughter of an impoverished Polish nobleman. The union was agreed on four main conditions: that he enter the Catholic church; that the marriage would not be solemnized until he was crowned; that he promise to bring Russia into the Catholic church; and that he reward the Mniszek family with enormous estates and wealth.

Boris, after a rapid decline, died suddenly from unknown causes. Although the King of Poland withdrew his troops from the Pretender's army when it crossed into Russia, a rabble swelled his forces. Their advance had been halted at Kromy by the Tsar's generals, when news of Boris's death was brought.

In the ensuing years of chaos, Fyodor and his mother were killed; Xenia was raped and forced to become a nun. Grigory reigned with Marina for less than a year before he was murdered. Shuisky followed him as Tsar but was forced to abdicate. The 'Time of Troubles' only ended in 1613 when the Romanovs established the dynasty which was to last until 1917.

The Drama and Music of 'Boris'

Laurel E. Fay

Boris Godunov, Mussorgsky's only completed opera, stands as a monument to the composer's ideal of a 'realistic' musical drama. Capitalizing on the lessons learned from work on his unfinished opera, *The Marriage*, Mussorgsky succeeded in *Boris* in rendering 'the straightforward expression of thoughts and feelings as it occurs in ordinary speech' in a manner that is both musically and dramatically convincing.

The drama of *Boris Godunov* is highly unusual. Much of the opera's action occurs not on the stage, but behind the scenes. What we see on stage are the personal and psychological reactions of the participants to the historical events, as interpreted by Mussorgsky and his sources. Like Pushkin, Mussorgsky expected his audience to know the events which frame the drama, and his opera provides an open-ended commentary on them. The exact nature and extent of that commentary depends greatly on whether Mussorgsky's first or second version is adopted and on innumerable details of production and interpretation. Nevertheless, some features remain constant. Mussorgsky adapts from Pushkin the fundamental conflict between earthly 'power' and spiritual 'humility'. Both Boris and Dimitry fall prey to the former and the tragedy of Boris is that his lust for power has corrupted him beyond hope of salvation. While we see only the seeds of Dimitry's downfall, we are provided with many signposts to indicate that his fate will be analogous. The opposition of these extremes can be seen clearly in the characters of Pimen and Rangoni. The former, having renounced worldy life, attains an enviable peace and tranquility. The latter, manipulating his religious power to achieve political ends, is an embodiment of pure evil. While the role of Shuisky — the scheming boyar — is seemingly minor, he nevertheless serves as a wilful catalyst for the psychological destruction of Boris. However, he too is doomed. The simpleton, or 'holy fool', is blessed with spiritual insight. It is left to him to predict, with devastating precision, the fate of the nation.

Underlying the personal tragedies is the more pervasive tragedy of the Russian nation and its people. They play an active role in the drama. Though the people are ignorant and sometimes misguided, it is their misery and suffering which ultimately crush Boris.

The complex drama has a roughly symmetrical structure. At the beginning of the opera — or at least by the Coronation scene — we see Boris at the height of his power. Through the course of the opera we witness his decline into despair, madness and, finally, death. When we first see Grigory, he is an obscure novice in a monastery. By the end of the opera he has assumed the identity of the Tsarevich Dimitry and, nearing the pinnacle of his power, he marches towards Moscow. The paths of their destinies cross almost imperceptibly. Boris never meets his avenger. In fact, in the original version of the opera, Grigory is not seen again after he escapes acorss the Lithuanian border and becomes the Pretender. Nevertheless, the threat he poses continues to shadow Boris by means of the musical leitmotif associated with him.

The musical treatment is unconventional. Mussorgsky renounces the traditional forms and techniques of operatic writing. His score is not divided into arias, recitatives and so on, but evolves continuously. He allows little scope for purely vocal display and virtuosity. The declamation corresponds to the rhythms and inflections of the spoken language remarkably closely. The harmonies, frequently modal, do not conform to the standards of Mussorgsky's Western contemporaries and are more reminiscent of Rusian folk music.

The influence of folk music is important in the opera. While there are relatively few real folk tunes in the score, Mussorgsky had an extraordinary flair for capturing the flavour of folk music in his own melodies and this is nowhere more evident than in the score of *Boris Godunov*.

Musical unity in the opera is achieved primarily through the use of a series of leitmotifs, reflecting both characters and their emotions. While the motif associated with Dimitry [9] is undoubtedly the most common example, many others contribute to the expressiveness and continuity of the drama.

Prologue

Scene One. The first measures of the opera are stamped with the hallmarks of Mussorgsky's 'folk' style. The opening theme [1], played by unaccompanied bassoons, is comprised of short phrases, a narrow melodic range focussing on the tonic and subdominant, a flexible rhythmic structure, and the modal colouring of a lowered leading tone. As the theme shifts successively to violas, clarinet, cellos and bassoons, it remains essentially unchanged. Using a technique favoured by Russian composers in folk-song settings, Mussorgsky achieves variety by changing the 'background' or accompaniment figurations in each appearance.

As the curtain rises and the brief introduction comes to an end, trombones pave the way for an ominous semi-quaver motif [2]. While the motif is associated here with Nikitich, the police officer, it can be associated more broadly with the forces of oppression and coercion which underlie the scene. By means of brusque commands and threats, Nikitich goads the rabble outside the monastery into a kneeling prayer of supplication to Boris: 'Why forsake us and leave us helpless, great boyar?' [3]. The sighing melodic phrases, particularly on the words 'Pity us!' underline the wretchedness of their condition. But the real ambivalence of their attitude becomes clear in the episode which follows when, freed from police supervision, individual complaints are voiced and eventually degenerate into confused bickering. Trombone blasts and the semi-quaver motif signal the abrupt reappearance of Nikitich and, cowed into submission once more, the crowd repeats its supplication. This time the prayer, accompanied by a variant of the 'oppression' motif, takes on an ironic and somewhat mechanical quality.

Shchelkalov's speech announcing Boris's rejection of the proffered crown is a model of Mussorgsky's 'realistic' vocal writing. The simple melodic and rhythmic inflections, against a sparse orchestral accompaniment, serve to emphasize the emotional tone of the text. At the climax, Shchelkalov intones on Eb —his highest pitch – the words 'Disaster has come, disaster for all of us, O ye Orthodox!' With a shift from the minor to major mode, he prays that 'heavenly wisdom' be sent to Boris. As if to reinforce this plea, a chorus of blind pilgrims appears singing a hymn glorifying God and praying for Russia's salvation [4]. By means of the voice-leading — the manner in which the individual lines in the texture unfold — and the harmonic progressions, Mussorgsky effectively simulates the style of Orthodox choral music. In many productions the scene draws to a close as the pilgrims enter the monastery and their hymn dies away, but Mussorgsky's original version of the opera includes an additional episode in which members of the crowd, accompanied by fragments of the opening theme and pilgrims' hymn, debate the meaning of the pilgrims' words. In a clever stroke, the question 'And who is our Tsar?' is immediately followed by the semi-quaver 'oppression' motif, and the musical association of the motif with the answer – 'It's Boris!' – becomes indelible. Nikitich hands out orders for the following day and, against a backdrop of fragments from the opening theme, the crowd disperse in a mood of grumbling resignation.

Scene Two. Popularized through Rimsky-Korsakov's version, Mussorgsky's own orchestration of the 'Coronation' scene may appear, at first, drab by comparison. In addition to his extensive musical modifications, Rimsky-Korsakov fitted out the scene with a more brilliant and lavish scoring than that of Mussorgsky. But the composer's more restrained orchestration serves a dramatic function: in a manner more consistent with the first scene, it casts a shadow on the festive atmosphere of the coronation.

Nevertheless, Mussorgsky's orchestration of the resounding Kremlin bells at the beginning of the scene [5a] is one of the most inspired achievements in the history of music. By alternating, in the brass instruments, dominant seventh chords a tritone apart (on Ab and D), accompanied by offbeat strokes in the tuba, tam-tam and basses, Mussorgsky creates an unforgettably graphic imitation of the ancient bells. The addition of higher-pitched instruments and gradually increased rhythmic activity helps to build the tension and excitement. As the curtain rises the 'bells' break off and the cycle begins again, this time accompanied by 'a great peal of bells on stage', and the imposing visual spectacle of the procession of guards, Streltsy, boyars and other dignitaries. A trumpet fanfare, Prince Shuisky's acclamation of the new Tsar, and a flourish in the strings lead to the choral song 'Like the sun in the skies, supreme in its glory' [6]. This is one of relatively few 'borrowed' folk melodies in the opera. In fact, it was also used by other 19th-century composers, most notably by Beethoven in the second of his 'Razumovsky' quartets, op. 59 no. 2.

As Boris appears on the cathedral porch, he is hailed by thunderous cries of 'Glory!', but the clamour dies away to a hush and the mood of celebration is dissipated by the foreboding motif which introduces Boris's soliloquy [7]. He

Richard Van Allan in the 1980 ENO production (photo: Reg Wilson)

19

Inia Te Wiata as Pimen. (photo: Donald Southern; Covent Garden Archives)

confesses that his soul is tormented by a secret terror and, accompanied by shimmering *tremolo* strings, he prays for God's forgiveness. Dispelling his gloomy thoughts and regaining his majestic stance, Boris invites everyone to a feast and is greeted with renewed shouts of 'Glory!' The on-stage bells resume, as does the choral song of rejoicing. Triplets and cross-rhythms enhance the exciting conclusion.

Approximately five years separate the action of the Prologue from that of the rest of the opera.

Act One

Scene One. The opening bars set the prevailing mood for the scene in 'A Cell in the Chudov Monastery'. Gently undulating seconds in the violas, punctuated by chords of open fifths, ingeniously evoke both the tranquil hours of early morning and the unhurried motion of Pimen's writing. Pimen's vocal line, as befits the pious monk, is simple and unaffected. As he becomes lost in thought, the strings play a motif which will reappear thoughout the scene [8]. It is associated with Pimen's reflections and the events of his secular past.

Pimen patiently continues his chronicle and the undulating seconds continue as an off-stage chorus of monks quietly intones a prayer. The novice Grigory awakes and marvels at Pimen's perseverance and wisdom. Attracting Pimen's attention, Grigory asks for his blessing which, in an ironic twist, is delivered as the off-stage monks sing 'Why, O Lord my God, hast Thou forsaken me?' Grigory relates his prophetic dream of climbing to the top of a lofty tower – suitably illustrated by the rising vocal line – being mocked by the people of Moscow and falling. Pimen advises the youth to calm his passions with prayer and admits, accompanied by an aggressive statement of his motif, that he too sometimes dreams of 'wild and wanton feasts, skirmishes and battles'. Grigory envies the excitement of Pimen's boyhood and, using Pimen's motif, asks 'Why cannot I enjoy the thrill of war . . .?' But Pimen endorses the renunciation of worldly life and cites the cases of previous tsars as confirmation. His tone changes when he comes to Boris and he grimly asserts 'we must endure [an] accursed regicide as Tsar!'

In his second version of the opera, Mussorgsky cut Pimen's lengthy description of the murder of Tsarevich Dimitry which follows. It is here, however, that the first glimpses of the 'Dimitry' motif [9], which plays such an important role throughout the rest of the opera, can be found. In the shortened second version, the motif makes its appearance as Pimen calculates 'He'd be as old as you are and reign today!' Thereafter, this leitmotif is inseparably connected with the figure of the dead Tsarevich and his re-incarnated counterpart.

The bell for matins rings. After Grigory has escorted the ageing monk to the door, he defiantly condemns Boris to face the judgement of the people and God.

Scene Two. After an instrumental introduction foreshadowing themes to be heard later, the scene at 'An Inn on the Lithuanian Border' opens with the Hostess singing an engaging song about a duck [10]. Newly composed for the second version its repeated angular phrases, text and stanza structure nonetheless give it a folk quality. An *ostinato* figure in the bass signals the approach of potential customers and the Hostess breaks off her song only to resume it after the false alarm. Varlaam and Missail, vagabond monks, are heard outside begging unctuously for alms [11] and the Hostess scurries to make ready for her visitors. They enter accompanied by Grigory, now the pretender-to-be Dimitry and associated throughout with the characteristic motif. Varlaam impatiently orders wine, begins to drink, and launches into the rousing *Ballad of Kazan* [12].

In his play, Pushkin specified the names of Varlaam's two songs in this scene, but melodies proved difficult to locate. Accordingly, for the *Ballad of Kazan* Mussorgsky composed an original tune in the folk manner, with two repeated phrases, the first in the phrygian mode and the second in a minor key. The exotic flourishes which introduce the song and the changing instrumentation and harmonies for each verse help convey a vivid dramatic quality to the tale. Having berated Grigory for his sobriety, Varlaam begins his second song, 'He walks along' [13], while sprawling on the table. Mussorgsky adapted an existent folk song to this text and the repeated notes, narrow melodic range and generally lethargic pace are ideally suited to portray the sleepy and drunken monk. In one of the rare ensemble sections of the opera, Grigory engages the Hostess in whispered consultations as Varlaam sporadically continues his song. Knocking is heard but, with a humourous musical touch, Varlaam hears it as part of his dream. The reappearance of the ominous 'oppression' motif [2] in the strings identifies the newcomers as policemen. They suspiciously investigate the clientele and Varlaam tries to ingratiate himself by lamenting the sorry state of Christian charity.

The police-officer has focussed his suspicions on Varlaam, however, and Grigory helpfully agrees to read their warrant, substituting a description of Varlaam for his own. Underlying the description of Grigory's crimes we hear a reference to Boris's motif of foreboding from the Coronation scene [7]. Outraged by the cruel joke, Varlaam grabs the warrant and haltingly begins to decipher the words to the melody of his second song. As he gains confidence his pace picks up and his pitch gradually ascends, but his reading is still comically stilted. When it finally becomes clear who the real culprit is, Grigory is able to escape during the pandemonium.

Act Two

The single scene in this act gives us our first extended profile of the character of Boris and the conflicts which torment him. For the second version of his opera Mussorgsky revised and expanded this scene greatly, incorporating — among other details suggested by his research into Karamzin's *History of the Russian State* — the folk-like songs sung by the Nurse and Fyodor, and the chiming clock. The former help to throw Boris's suffering into sharp relief and the latter provides a visual and aural focus for his hallucination.

The scene opens as Xenia laments the death of her fiancé [14]. Fyodor tries to

Alexander Pirogov as Boris and Nikolai Khaniev as Shuisky. (Stuart-Liff Collection)

comfort her but is distracted by the chiming and movement of the clock, its mechanism rendered in the swirling chromatic phrases of the violins. The Nurse, with her earthy wisdom, then tries to console Xenia and sings a lively song about a gnat [15]. As in so much folk lore, what starts out as a cheerful story ends morbidly, and to dispel the mood Fyodor offers a clapping song with nonsensical lyrics [16]. Nurse joins in enthusiastically but cries out in fright when she catches sight of Boris. The Tsar comforts Xenia; his sympathy is mirrored in tender phrases [17]. He then watches proudly as his son demonstrates his knowledge of the map of Russia [18], and becomes lost in reflection.

Boris emerges as a tragic and pathetic figure in his monologue. Despite his power, he is tormented [19] and nothing can console him, not even his children [17]. The sorrowful *andante* which follows – 'How fearful is the wrath of God on high' [20] – emphasizes the anguish of his guilty soul. As he admits that his sleep is troubled by visions of a blood-stained child, an eerie chromatic descent of triplets is heard [21]. A commotion breaks out and Boris sends Fyodor to investigate. Meanwhile a boyar announces the arrival of Prince Shuisky and denounces him as a traitor. Before he turns his attention to this serious matter, Boris patiently and lovingly listens to his son's tale about a parrot which disturbed the nurses [22]. Accompanied by Fyodor's motif from earlier in the scene [18], Boris warns the future monarch against the treachery of men like Shuisky.

Shuisky himself enters and, over a menacing pedal tone, Boris furiously accuses him of sedition. Shuisky tries to insinuate himself back into the Tsar's favour by revealing the news that a Pretender has appeared in Poland. Boris anxiously demands his name but Shuisky prolongs the suspense with an ingratiating profession of loyalty. When he finally identifies the Pretender he sings the 'Dimitry' motif [9]. Boris is stunned and, hastening Fyodor from the room, orders Shuisky to take appropriate measures to protect the realm. But he holds him back. Here the Tsar's fear is reflected in another motif of chromatic triplets [23]. He needs to assure himself that the child who was murdered in Uglich really was Dimitry. With an ingenuously simple musical accompaniment Shuisky describes, in cruel detail, the features of the dead prince. Boris can stand no more. As he waves Shuisky away the motif of his fear reappears.

Boris is choking with emotion as the clock begins to chime again. The sounds of the clock's mechanism, which earlier were a source of wonderment to Fyodor, serve here only to echo and intensify Boris's physical and spiritual pain. The poison of guilt 'throbs and throbs' within him. Suddenly horror-struck, he sees the apparition of Dimitry from his dream [21]. In a broken voice he frantically tries to exorcise the apparition and, as the scene ends, the shattered man begs for God's mercy.

Act Three

The two scenes of Act Three were added by Mussorgsky to the second version of his opera. By introducing the character of Marina Mniszek, the proud Polish princess, he injected a romantic element into the opera. Perhaps more importantly, by his depiction of the wily Jesuit priest, Rangoni – who had no prototype in Pushkin – and by demonstrating the power he holds over both Marina and Dimitry, Mussorgsky pointed the way to the inevitable clash between

Irina Archipova as Marina. (Stuart-Liff Collection)

Elizabeth Connell (Marina) and Geoffrey Chard (Rangoni) in the 1980 ENO production. (photo: Reg Wilson)

Catholicism and Orthodoxy and for Dimitry's ultimate downfall. The music of this Act is distinguished stylistically from the rest by its greater refinement and elegance, as well as by the use of stereotypical Polish features such as the dotted rhythms and syncopations of the mazurka and the stately polonaise. Mussorgsky thus uses musical means to effect a national distinction.

Scene One. While a chorus of maidens sings her praises [24], Marina has her hair arranged. She, however, would prefer songs of Poland's martial glory. In a melody marked by its dotted rhythms and accented weak beats [25], she confesses that her days are full of endless tedium. Only Dimitry, and the Russian throne to which he aspires, have any attraction for her. She is determined to conquer both. The sudden appearance of Rangoni startles her, but she listens in humility as he describes the wretched state of the Church [26]. Seeing Marina's distress, Rangoni presses his advantage and tells her that she must 'convert the faithless crowd of Moscow!' Marina is momentarily flattered and overwhelmed by the prospect he sets before her. Accompanied by a sinister descending chromatic scale [27], Rangoni tells her that she can and must bewitch the Pretender with her beauty. He encourages her, in a melody marked by its insinuating chromatic intervals [28], to use all her feminine wiles to entrap Dimitry, ignoring her conscience, and make him swear allegiance to Rome [27]. Marina is appalled by his unscrupulous cynicism but Rangoni threatens her, over a menacing pedal tone, with hell's damnation. As she collapses in terror, he secures her obedience [27].

Scene Two. The addition of a harp to the orchestra imparts a romantic atmosphere to the moonlit scene in the garden of the Mniszek castle. The Pretender [9], captivated by Marina's charms, waits for her. Introduced by his sinister chromatic scale, Rangoni inflames him with tales of the humiliation that the lovesick Marina endures on his account. 'Dimitry' vows to make her Tsaritsa of Russia [9]. With affected candour, Rangoni assures him that he needs no payment for his services as match-maker, but a return of his insinuating motif [28] reveals his true intention when he begs to be allowed to advise 'Dimitry'. He persuades him, with difficulty, to hide from the approaching courtiers, who enter the garden to the strains of a polonaise [29]. As Marina flirts with an elderly nobleman, her guests celebrate the imminent conquest of Moscow.

After the polonaise has died away, 'Dimitry' returns, now doubting whether Marina really loves him. He is on the verge of departing at once for battle [9] when her sudden appearance melts his resolve and he confesses his love [30]. She haughtily teases him for his lovesickness and asks 'How soon will you reign in Moscow as the Tsar?' Only the throne of Russia can tempt her. Taunted beyond endurance, his pride asserts itself [9] and he declares that when he is Tsar he will have his revenge. It is now Marina's turn to plead, claiming that she goaded him intentionally – out of her love [32]. She quickly dispels his lingering doubts and, as the scene ends, Rangoni gloats over the credulous lovers [28].

Act Four

The initial version contained one scene that was not incorporated into the second version: 'A square in front of the Cathedral of Basil the Blessed in Moscow'. Many modern productions, however, while opting for the expanded second version, include this scene because it gives additional insight into the suffering of the Russian people and shows the confrontation between the Tsar and the simpleton.

At the beginning of the scene, a crowd of peasants mills outside the cathedral and discusses the enigmatic happenings inside. Their confusion, as well as some of the musical motifs, recalls the similar situation at the very beginning of the opera. They cannot understand why 'Grishka Otrepyev' has been cursed and many are convinced that Tsarevich Dimitry [9] is alive and marching towards Moscow. They shout 'To death with traitors, and to death with Tsar Boris!' before they are hushed. As they resume pacing and scratching their heads, a group of urchins swarms around a simpleton, as he sings a lament 'Moonlight's shining' [39]. The sighing, repetitive accompaniment and the disjointed vocal line effectively convey his simple-mindedness. When the urchins steal the silver kopek he has found, he begins to whine. Meanwhile the Tsar's retinue emerges from the church and, in a chorus again reminiscent of the first scene of the Prologue [3], the crowd plaintively begs for alms and bread. The crying simpleton attracts Boris's attention and asks him, with annihilating directness, to murder the boys 'just as you murdered Dimitry, the young Tsarevich'. Shuisky is about to seize him, but Boris — recognizing the holy source of his wisdom — gently asks for his prayers. The simpleton deals Boris a harsh blow when he rejects the request flatly, confiding ingenuously 'I must not pray for a Tsar Herod!' Repeating his melody of lament [39], the simpleton prophetically forecasts the misery and destruction which await Russia and her people. There can be no doubt that his predictions will be fulfilled.

In his second version, Mussorgsky worked the incident between the simpleton and the urchins, and the lament, into the final scene. When both scenes are performed, the redundant material is usually cut from the 'Kromy Forest' scene, with the exception of the simpleton's prophetic lament, which ends both.

Scene One. Boris's death scene owes much of its impact to the fact that it makes extensive use of motifs, and their corresponding emotional connotations, from earlier in the opera. The opening theme, however, is new and becomes associated with the Council of boyars [33]. Shchelkalov's entry is marked by a return of the music which introduced him in the first scene of the Prologue. As he begins to address the Council we hear a reminiscence of one of Boris's themes from Act Two [19]. Shchelkalov's voice gradually ascends as he reads the Tsar's

Adamo Didur who sang the title role in the American première in 1913. (Met. Archives)

Anne Pashley (Fyodor) embraced by Boris Christoff as the Tsar. (photo: Donald Southern)

proclamation. The boyars then debate [33] and dictate that the traitorous Pretender should be caught, tortured, hanged and desecrated. Their petty bickering, much like that of the peasants in earlier scenes, is droll. By contrast, the tragic nature of the events to follow is dramatically enhanced. Shuisky arrives, begging forgiveness for his lateness, but the other boyars suspect him of collusion with the Pretender [9]. He distracts them by describing, to their utter disbelief, the Tsar's morbid condition. When he describes the hallucination, his story receives grim confirmation by the appearance of Boris, dishevelled and violently agitated, fleeing from the apparition evoked by the music [21] — a flash-back to the end of Act Two. Finally regaining his senses and recognizing his surroundings, Boris addresses the boyars and consents to see a holy man who craves audience, hoping that he will bring much-needed words of consolation. In a stroke of genius, Mussorgsky departed from Pushkin's original to allow Pimen [8] to be the unsuspecting and ironic instrument of Boris's final collapse, also providing another strand of continuity to the drama. Pimen relates a tale of a miracle worked at the tomb of the Tsarevich Dimitry [9]. As the tale unfolds Boris grows increasingly restless and agitated until he can bear no more. He falls with a shriek [21]. The boyars rush to his aid and summon Fyodor.

The Tsarevich runs in [18] and, embracing him, Boris solemnly imparts his final instructions. Recalling — through leitmotifs — poignant images from the second Act, he cautions his son to beware of the Pretender [9] and scheming boyars, to protect the faith and his sister Xenia [17]. After Boris invokes Heaven's blessing for his innocent children, a gloomy reminder of the coronation bells is heard in the death knell. Hearing the funeral dirge approach, Boris asks for sackcloth so that he may end his life as a monk. Even this comfort, however, is denied him. The words of the chant, speaking of the death of a little child, bring further agony to Boris and when he hears 'but there is no salvation', he rises and cries imperiously 'I am still Tsar!' This effort consumes his energy and he

Nicolai Ghiaurov at Covent Garden. (photo: Donald Southern)

collapses. With his dying breath he points to Fyodor as the new Tsar and whispers in anguish, 'forgive me!' The scene ends with a wistful reminder of the motif associated with Boris's tormented soul [19].

Scene Two. The scene, in 'a clearing in a forest near Kromy', was the third new scene added to the second version. In many respects it provides an ironic parallel to the Coronation scene. The people have switched their allegiance to Dimitry and hail him as enthusiastically as they formerly greeted Boris. Swirling string passages [36] emphasize their unruliness as they drag in the captured boyar Krushchov. He is gagged and a guard is mounted. An old hag is found as a 'suitable' sweetheart for him and the crowd taunts their captive with a folk song, 'Like a falcon that's chained in captivity' [37]. This song is one of several in the scene which Mussorgsky borrowed or adapted from traditional sources. Its verses

William McAlpine as the Pretender in the Covent Garden production. (photo: Houston Rogers)

alternate with mocking praise: 'Honour the great boyar, slave of our wicked Tsar' [38]. The incident between the simpleton and the urchins, transferred from the 'St Basil scene', now takes place (see above), but the simpleton's crying is cut short by Varlaam and Missail, singing [40]. Denouncing the crimes of Boris, they stir the mob into a frenzy: 'Casting off our chains of bondage, we shall set our people free' [41]. When two Jesuits appear, chanting – in Latin – their support for Dimitry, the crowd turns its fury on them and decides to hang 'the blood-sucking vampires'. As they are dragged away, martial strains and trumpet calls are heard and the Pretender arrives, hailed by the monks and the crowd. 'Dimitry' grants clemency to Krushchov and summons the crowd to take arms in his cause [9]. The two Jesuits join in the triumphant procession. As it fades away — visually and musically — the simpleton is left alone in the clearing, with flames from a burning village visible in the distance. He sings his pathetic lament [39], weeping for the fate of the Russian people. The frequently tempestuous music of this crowd scene throws the simplicity of the simpleton's song into sharp relief. This overwhelming contrast underscores the conflicts of the entire drama with its opposition of earthly 'power' and spiritual 'humility'. The simpleton, with his mournful prophecy, has the last word. The music dies away to alternating pitches of a minor second and the drama is left unresolved. The 'time of troubles' has only just begun . . .

Around 'Boris Godunov'

Alex de Jonge

The period described by historians as 'the time of troubles' has made a particularly deep impression upon the Russian historical imagination. It represents the nadir of disorder, that political disorder feared so greatly that the crack of firm, very firm, government is often considered a preferable alternative. The time of troubles not only produced four tsars of Russia in just over a year, it also witnessed the occupation of Holy and Orthodox Moscow by Catholic Poles, an event which subsequent generations of Russians have looked upon somewhat askance: Napoleon was bad enough, but Poles . . . ? It was also a time which provided plenty of what Pushkin in another context called 'Russian rebellion, pitiless and senseless'. The troubles provided the inspiration for the first major Russian opera, Glinka's *Life for the Tsar*. It tells the story of Ivan Susanin who saved the life of the first Romanov tsar Mikhail Fedorovich when he was being pursued by a band of marauding Poles; Susanin lured them away only to be killed himself when they realised what he had done. Before his death he sang the splendid aria 'They guess the truth' — '*chuyut pravdu*', one of Chaliapin's favourite passages. A magnificent celebration of Russian patriotism, and of the Romanovs too, the opera was chosen for a special gala to commemorate the tricentenary of the dynasty in 1913. Members of the diplomatic corps unfamiliar with the opera, and also those who knew it well and eagerly awaited Chaliapin's performance as Susanin, found the gala version of the opera somewhat puzzling. In order to spare the sensibilities of a Poland which had the dubious good fortune to be a part of the Russian Empire at that time, the director had been instructed to omit the scene of the murder, even though this constituted the climax of the opera. Bureaucratic interference in the arts is a tradition long established in mother Russia.

The death of the tsarevich Dimitry in Uglich has its own special significance in Russian history. Such is its resonance that the mere name Uglich is enough to evoke the whole atmosphere of the time of troubles, the poet Osip Mandelstam using it in precisely this way in one of his finest poems. The cause of the tsarevich's death constitutes one of the enduring riddles of Russian history. Although Mussorgsky, in the wake of Pushkin and Karamzin, concludes unequivocally that the child was murdered by Godunov's assassins, there is a respectable school of thought which maintains that he died by accident, 'while playing with a knife'. Admittedly this does rather remind one of the kind of unfortunate victim who accidentally falls to his death through a window in the headquarters of the KGB, nonetheless the question remains an open one. The theme of the murdered tsarevich occurs with subtle variations in many periods of Russian history. It actually begins before the death of Dimitry, with Ivan the Terrible's accidental killing of his own son. It is then repeated when Peter the Great has his firstborn flogged and tortured to death. There are further variations in the eighteenth century when Catherine the Great condones the murder of her husband, Peter III, while her own son Paul I was killed with the probable connivance of his son, the future Alexander I. The theme is given a grandiose rendering when the entire Imperial family was assassinated by the Bolsheviks in 1918, and has further delicate elaboration at the hands of Stalin. He may or may not have been responsible for the death of his wife — there was a lot of suicide about in the 1930's — and did remarkably little to prevent his elder son from being killed in a German POW camp.

Along with the theme of the dead tsarevich, the story of Dimitry and Boris

Ivan Petrov as Boris and Ivan Koslovsky as the Simpleton. (Stuart-Liff Collection)

produces yet another protagonist who seems peculiarly typical of Russian history — the pretender Grishka Otrepyev, the false tsar, and the first of a series of persons claiming to be the true Dimitry. It has been suggested that the remarkable role played by pretenders in the Russian popular imagination, a role extending well beyond the Revolution, derives from the people's deep-seated longing for liberation and justice in the face of arbitrary and oppressive rule. For centuries there was a widespread belief in a mythical 'true tsar', the descendant of the apparently extinct Rurik line. He lay hidden somewhere in the heart of Russia, but one day would reveal himself, overthrow his enemies and bring about a golden age when all would be treated fairly and be freed from the nobility and the false tsar who ruled illegitimately over Russia. Time and again the leaders of popular rebellions such as Stenka Razin in the 17th century, or Pugachev in the 18th, would claim that they were the true tsar who would lead their people to freedom, and were accorded the appropriate honours by their supporters. As late as the 1890's there could be found peasants who claimed to be descendants and heirs of Pugachev, bearing the 'marks of the tsar' upon their chest. Many years later, in the 1940's, Solzhenitsyn shared a Moscow prison cell with an ex-chauffeur who had worked in the Kremlin and who claimed that when he was a child a mysterious old man of venerable countenance had appeared and told him that he was not just any ordinary Soviet schoolboy but was in reality Michael the future emperor of all the Russias.

Together with this belief in quasi-mythical potential rulers went the suspicion that an unpopular tsar was not the real tsar at all, but a substitute. Substitution was often effected by witchcraft. Thus it was rumoured that the real Peter the Great had been spirited away by a wicked sorceress who first roasted him in an iron pan and then kept him in a house of glass; in his stead there reigned a cloven-footed stand-in who was none other than Antichrist. At a much later date, in early 1918 in fact, it was rumoured among the peasants of the lower Volga that the last tsarevich, Aleksey, would prove the salvation of Russia, for he was really the son of Rasputin so that at length there would come a tsar with the blood of a Russian peasant in his veins.

As he matured Pushkin grew increasingly interested in what he saw to be the key episodes in the forging of the Russian cultural identity. Along with Peter the Great, whom he celebrated ambiguously in *The Bronze Horseman* and more conventionally in *Poltava*, he studied periods of disorder, such as the Pugachev rebellion, the subject of a historical study and a novel, *The Captain's Daughter*. It is scarcely surprising that he should also turn to the time of troubles and the curiously ambiguous figure of Boris Godunov, for the subject offered such a rich collection of elements central to Russian historical mythology. The play that resulted has been subjected to much wagging of the academic finger and the kind of considered opinion that gives academic criticism a bad name. 'Interesting but flawed' goes the verdict of donnish common sense. Perhaps Pushkin himself might agree that the play was a failure, in that it failed to achieve his ambition of 'influencing the reform of our dramatic system'. However he can scarcely be blamed for that. There was in effect little enough system to reform and besides romantic historical drama may have had its moments, but it was essentially a dead end. Nevertheless it cannot be denied that along with Schiller, Grillparzer and de Musset's uniquely successful *Lorenzaccio, Boris Godunov* is one of the finest examples of this not very satisfactory and bookish genre; infinitely superior for example, to anything written by Hugo. There is, incidentally, a strong case to be made for the view that the most satisfactory aspect of romantic drama was its provision of raw material for the operas of Verdi and Mussorgsky.

To be fair to sensible critical opinion there is much about the play that is not satisfactory. It lacks the inexorable development of dramatic necessity. In this respect it is less a tragedy than a kind of pageant or chronicle moving from one eloquent or interesting scene to another. Pushkin brilliantly conveys the feel of the period creating a gorgeous sense of essential Russianness, something a little beyond the scope of academic or indeed any other kind of common sense. It does fail though to show the workings of a dramatic nemesis. But this is not really the fault of Pushkin. Sadly history is not always dramatically organised and we have to reconcile ourselves to the fact that Boris died, not as a result of his misdeeds coming home to roost, but of natural causes. His death was undoubtedly untimely, but a cause for sadness rather than tragedy. Tragedy comes later with the rapid dispatch of Godunov's offspring, but once Boris is gone it is all over bar the murdering, and Mussorgsky is right to bring the curtain down when he did. Moreover his musical elaboration of the deathbed scene, the instructions to his son and his choking plea for forgiveness do succeed in creating a tragic atmosphere splendidly pictured for us by Chaliapin who always considered Boris his greatest role:

> In spite of his despotism the wretched king is like a wounded lion surrounded by jackals and hyenas, who finally succeed in destroying him. For a time, instinctively feeling his power and dreading it, the boyars prowl

A sketch by Buchkin of Chaliapin as Varlaam. (Stuart-Liff Collection)

about him with hangdog glances and gnashing teeth. But only for a time. When the moment is ripe the treacherous and cowardly crowd tears the lion to pieces. Here again the Russian temperament is overwhelmingly manifest in the seditious licence of the boyars. . . It seems as though the Russian temperament is entirely devoid of moderation.

The second weakness with which Pushkin is charged is the inconsistency of his treatment of Grishka Otrepyev. At one moment he is a snivelling pretender cowering at the feet of the redoubtable Marina Mniszek, next he has all the dignity of a person who believes unquestioningly in his historic destiny. Yet some kind of a case can be made out even for these vacillations. Whatever else he might have been he was most emphatically not the strong leader that would take Russia into a stable future, and so Pushkin has him vacillate accordingly. In one respect he is strangely similar to Boris himself. Neither man is tsar by legitimate right. Both are aware that they have usurped their power, and for both this knowledge makes for a fundamental political gracelessness which prevents them from becoming the good and responsible ruler that each would like to be. Of course there is more than this to Boris, who is a relatively complex character. He is given an obvious Shakespearean colouring as a guilty ruler with blood on his hands: Pushkin makes him closer to Macbeth than Richard III. He is also endowed with considerable political wisdom and far-sightedness which emerge in his dying instructions to his son. This suggests a degree of political sophistication in the author that is remarkable when one recalls that Pushkin was only twenty-six when he wrote his play. It is less a case of his own political maturity than of a brilliant ear which was able to hear and re-create the tone appropriate to that kind of discourse, thereby convincing us that he is imparting observations of great political wisdom.

Indeed one of the towering strengths of Pushkin's play is the richness and variety of its tones. What he referred to as the 'truth of conversations' — 'istina razgovorov' — was almost his prime requirement as a dramatist. He wanted people to speak according to their character and position, considering the undifferentiated discourse of French classical drama a source of dreary textural blandness. In his play he goes lovingly, but economically, through a whole range of tones, from the archaic language of the old boyars to the strange folk idiom with its echo of thieves' cant spoken by the wandering monks. Each character has his own voice and sappy linguistic flavour. Admittedly such stylistic subtleties disappear in any musical setting more elaborate than the discreetest *intermezzo*. However the wide range covered by the characters' speech is echoed and amplified by the equally rich range of musical styles and levels in Mussorgsky's score.

Pushkin, and Mussorgsky after him, are trying to do more than pick out certain episodes considered crucial to the course taken by Russian history. They are also trying to give us the feel of a long-lost world, the world of old Muscovy as yet unaffected by contact with the West. They give us a sense of its political structure, of its hierarchy of boyars with their traditional offices, of a relationship of church and state whereby the patriarch was virtually as powerful as the tsar himself. It is a late medieval world which will finally be swept away by Peter the Great, and Russians have been arguing ever since about whether or not that was a good thing. Mussorgsky would take a second look at this period of transition (in a later phase) in *Khovanschina*. To Russian eyes and ears both versions of *Boris Godunov* are, along with their other virtues, magnificent celebrations of a certain kind of essential Russianness, and that is why they lie beyond the reach of carping criticism. Of course they deal with the majesty of autocracy, but they also give plenty of place to that entity known as the mighty Russian people, in some of its most curious manifestations.

We are introduced to a number of interesting Russian 'types'. Some require little explanation, since they have approximate counterparts in European history. Thus the character of Pimen the chronicler monk, who is somewhat mysteriously both protagonist and author of the chronicle we witness, does not call for much comment. The boyars too are approximately comparable to the European nobility, although they were more directly dependant upon their ruler in some respects, while the position one boyar family enjoyed *vis à vis* another was established by a bewilderingly elaborate series of books of precedence which determined who sat where and who was served when at banquets, and less satisfactorily, who served under whom in time of war. It is precisely this kind of institution that would vanish in the course of the seventeenth century.

Some of the popular characters will be less familiar. One of the most notable is the Simpleton. The Russian word *yurodiviy* is variously translated as simpleton, holy fool, fool in Christ. He was a familiar figure in pre-revolutionary Russia, one of many survivals from an earlier age. Although some simpletons were genuine half-witted beggars, many more were persons who had elected to adopt the course of abdication of reason as a form of heroic action. They would sacrifice their reason in order to practice humility and honour God. They were accorded the same respect that the Middle Ages gave to lunatics as persons enjoying a very special kind of Divine Favour, and were protected, venerated and supported accordingly. They were sometimes credited with the gift of tongues. Take Mitya Kolyaba, a crippled half-wit of the early 20th century who was supposed to utter prophecies in the course of his epileptic fits, 'when his voice changed from an uncanny whimper into the sinister howling of an animal. Finally it would become an unnerving and fear-inspiring roaring and braying'. His escort would interpret these sounds as prophecies uttered in strange tongues such as 'the language of Jerusalem'. Not all simpletons were so inarticulate. The most famous of them all, Basil the Blessed, was the only man who dared to speak the truth to Ivan the Terrible, and who went unpunished — Pushkin echoes the situation when the simpleton reminds Boris of his guilt. The episode is set on Red Square, in front of St Basil's Cathedral. Its official name is the Cathedral of the Intercession. But in 1588 a small chapel was erected next to the cathedral over the grave of the simpleton Basil, and the cathedral has borne his name ever since. (We are

Ezio Pinza as Boris at the Met. in 1938.
(Ida Cook Collection)

incidentally lucky that the cathedral still stands. It was very nearly removed in the 1930's to facilitate the flow of traffic on May Day Parades.) Traditionally simpletons should wear hair shirts, penitential chains and steel caps. In 1914 one observer counted no less than seven simpletons in the town of Novgorod alone, steel caps and all.

The second set of quintessentially Russian characters of a popular kind are the wandering monks that we see with Grishka in the inn. The *strannik* or wanderer was another enduring feature of Russian life, again a medieval survival. They were essentially pilgrims, wandering across the face of Russia from one holy place to another, saving their souls and avoiding regular work. The pilgrimage could last for months, years or indefinitely, becoming a way of life. They would procede from village to village providing tales of their travels or recipes for the saving of one's soul in exchange for board and lodging. The routes to the great monasteries would be crowded with such persons from dawn to dusk. Often a man would up and leave his secular life, abandoning his land or business to his children, and set off on the road to save his soul. Perhaps the most famous, or notorious, of all Russian pilgrims was Rasputin, who spent some ten years on the road before entering history. Chaliapin writes with extraordinary penetration and eloquence about the wanderers, when discussing the character of Varlaam, which Mussorgsky develops so beautifully with his melancholy bass line. For Chaliapin the wanderers were driven by a search for justice, for a land where life might prove kinder, or else they were simply trying to escape from themselves, from the *toska* or nostalgic melancholy which he feels to be fundamentally, essentially Russian. Varlaam is the very embodiment of the wanderer:

> Mussorgsky, with passionate intensity has succeeded in expressing the illimitable soul sickness of the pilgrim. So overwhelming is Varlaam's *toska* that he must either hang himself or laugh till he dies during the frenzied orgy.

He goes on to describe a character tortured by a sense of his own worthlessness. He sees himself as doomed, useless, rotten, and consequently develops a terrible indifference to his own fate; indifference is the source both of his courage and his endurance. In order to seek relief from that indifference he turns to drink or to compulsive wandering, but nothing can ever cure the sickness that lies in his spirit.

Whether one considers the play or the opera, the rich choral singing outside the Novodyevichy monastery or Pimen's loving monologues, the conclusion is the same. The true hero of these works is the Russian people itself, in a variety of manifestations. It has served for many émigrés as a kind of *Russie portative*, the embodiment of a certain transportable essence of Russia. Although compact and handy such essences can make for dangerous oversimplifications, and the tendency to quote Pushkin and say 'it breathes of Russia' with a catch in one's throat is splendidly guyed by Nabokov who satirises a slightly different idealised Russia consisting of 'the Red Army, an anointed monarch, collective farms, anthroposophy, the Russian Church and the Hydro-Electric Dam'. However there is one sense at least in which *Boris Godunov* captures something very close to the essence of Russian history. The action proper begins with the murder of one child, Dimitry, and ends with the murder of another, Godunov's son. Innocence is destroyed twice over, neither death changing anything, as if to suggest that history is no more than a series of cycles marked by the murder of innocents punctuating periods of misery and oppression for a long-suffering Russian people whose story can scarcely be considered to be a great and steady ascent towards the light.

Boris: prince or peasant?

A discussion of orchestration and style in two versions of 'Boris Godunov'

Nigel Osborne

Some artists may become legends in their time; Mussorgsky became a myth. His Russian contemporaries, like Rimsky-Korsakov, and above all Tchaikovsky, may have enjoyed recognition and acclaim in Europe's concert halls and opera houses, and even a measure of personal kudos and notoriety; Mussorgsky's achievement was less tangible, but arguably more far-reaching. Recognition was slow to come, but his influence seeped into the imaginations of fellow artists, and ultimately into the consciousness of his nation, in a special way, like a symbol, more a mythological than a historical figure.

How did this come about? Perhaps because Mussorgsky grew close to the Russian archetype of a visionary, a *yurodiviy* — like the simpleton in *Boris Godunov* — a simple soul, the village fool, possessed by demonic knowledge and creative powers. Mussorgsky was of course no idiot, but the erratic behaviour of his later life, his depressions and drunken spells and, above all, the quality of his work would have suggested this parallel to his more sober contemporaries. For the exacting craftsman/composer, like Rimsky-Korsakov, his music was suffused with vital and inspired substance, but poorly turned out, unbalanced and full of inaccuracies. It needed to be corrected and, like a myth, to be refined and modified before it could be passed on. So not only the *persona* but the works of Mussorgsky passed into mythology — no composer in recent history has been so often orchestrated, re-orchestrated and rewritten.

Of all Mussorgsky's myths *Boris Godunov* is surely both the most potent and the most reworked. It even began with something like a myth: a shady episode in Russian history, investigated by a Commission of Inquiry, recorded by Karamzin, turned into a poem by Pushkin and eventually shaped into a libretto by Mussorgsky himself. And in the form of an opera, its theme was to achieve a more timeless significance — the Russian fear of penetration from the West, and of the corruption of the pure Russian soul by Western sophistication — a piece of national psychology we ignore at our peril. Then came the reworkings, first by the composer himself, and then by Rimsky-Korsakov, Ippolitov-Ivanov and Shostakovich, not to mention the work of several editors. But of all these it is the version of Rimsky-Korsakov which has most communicated *Boris* to our own generation.

The revision came as an extension of a larger editorial project of preparing Mussorgsky's unfinished and 'imperfect' works for publication, which Rimsky undertook in the years following the composer's death in 1881. Its première in 1896, and performance in the subsequent years, served to relaunch the opera at a stage when the uneven momentum of its earlier success had drawn to a standstill. Most important of all, it came at a time when there emerged a generation of performers who seemed almost predestined for the roles — the young Chaliapin among them. So by a twist of fate — but perhaps, as we shall see, an inevitable one — Rimsky's version entered the repertoire as the real *Boris*.

Whatever criticisms Rimsky may have sustained for tampering with Mussorgsky's work, or standing in the way of the original, it is important that we do not misinterpret his motives. As Shostakovich pointed out, there are deep moral and ethical traditions in Russian music: a sense of community and mutual concern, at least within the artistic circle, which led to the selfless generosity of Rimsky and others towards fellow composers — towards the equally selfless Borodin, for example, or the young Stravinsky. Rimsky believed that his massive and time-consuming reworking of *Boris* was necessary to remove its 'solecisms' and to relaunch the opera on a sufficient scale and with adequate panache to capture the attention of an operatic milieu nurtured on grand opera, in the grips of a powerful star performer syndrome.

As the history of the twentieth century has been one of dismantling mythologies, so the quest for the real *Boris* has led to a long campaign to reinstate the Mussorgsky original. The Soviet scholar, Pavel Lamm, broke the ground in the 1920s, but not until 1975, and thanks to the brilliant and exhaustive work of David Lloyd-Jones, did a really comprehensive performing edition come within the grasp of the opera houses.

The fact that this edition has rapidly established itself in the repertoire seems to confirm Rimsky's own intuitions that there would come a time 'when the original is considered better and of greater value than my revision'. The 'competition' between these two versions serves to focus our attention on a fascinating conflict of values which resounds far beyond *Boris* itself. I believe it represents no less than one of the central crises of European art: the conflict between the professional and the primitive, the polished art product and a less choate originality, the rational control of a stable musical grammar and an intuitive exploration of latent possibilities.

Let us look more closely at these two versions. The main thrust of Rimsky's energies is directed towards orchestration; considering the brilliance and the sense of scale he achieves, it is surprising to discover that his orchestra differs from Mussorgsky's in only minor details, such as the addition of a third clarinet, doubling bass clarinet, or a triangle in the percussion section. We need look no further than the opening bars of the opera, however, to appreciate the differences in treatment. As the curtain is about to rise on the courtyard of the Novodievichy monastery, Mussorgsky presents the broad opening melody, a solemn folk-like tune, on first and second bassoon in unison; then the violas take up the same melody, in their middle register, over a flowing accompaniment in the cellos, doubled an octave lower by *pizzicato* basses. The effect in sound and atmosphere is sober, dark and somehow raw: there is something humble and unpretentious about it, a quality which pervades much of the opera. From one side it may even seem dull and plain, lacking brilliance — a criticism frequently levelled at Mussorgsky's orchestration; from another point of view, it may be seen as a positive and conscious aesthetic stand, in line with the nascent realism and rejection of showy 'art-for-art's-sake' apparent in Mussorgsky's generation of Russian artists. Here we inevitably cross the long shadow of the great social and literary critics of the nineteenth century, like Herzen, Chernishevsky or Dobrolyubov. If *Boris* provides some of the Russian heroes Dobrolyubov was waiting for, and the authentic cultural roots Herzen had advocated, it certainly embraces Chernishevsky's aesthetics (that art should closely imitate daily life and reality): in this, its orchestration is the humble cloak it wears.

Rimsky's version of the Prologue inhabits quite a different world. The opening statement is given to a single bassoon, doubled at the unison by cor Anglais, an instrument Rimsky himself described as having a 'listless, dreamy quality . . . sweet in the extreme'. So the melody takes on a *dolce ed espressivo* character, and arguably a heightened dramatic presence. The next statement of the melody is given to horns, doubled by clarinets, thus answering double reeds with a brass and woodwind combination at its most rounded and *legato*. Underneath, the accompaniment has lost its flowing quality, with *pizzicato* cellos giving it instead an elegant, 'walking-bass' feel. Not for the last time in the opera, Rimsky has shunned Mussorgsky's simple string-band writing, with its homogeneous 'choral' sound. Like Cui, he seemed allergic to the exposed string orchestra which pervades Mussorgsky's score, and in particular to the first version of the

Doboujinksy's design for the 'St Basil scene' at Sadler's Wells , when Mussorgsky's first version was performed with Ronald Stear as Boris and Laurance Collingwood conducting.

Polonaise, which he saw as an attempt to imitate a seventeenth century court band. (Ironically, Rimsky's first version of the Polonaise was scored for Wagnerian orchestra!) So throughout his orchestration, such passages are either totally recast, or subtly reinforced by the wind section. There are some exceptions, but these are for special dramatic effect, like the mournful ceremonial strings which accompany Boris as he dismisses the pining Xenia in Act Two.

Rimsky's orchestration seems to rest on two general principles. The first is one of timbral focus and brilliance, for which he and the Russian Nationalists became famous. The sensitive doublings of the opening of the Prologue find this at its most discreet. At the other end of the scale, one might cite Varlaam's song in Act One, scene two. Mussorgsky's instrumentation is shrill and rugged. Rimsky adds tubas and trombones to the stabbing bass line, and cymbals and bass drum to assert the rhythm; he also transposes the song from F♯ to F minor, possibly to facilitate sonorous string *pizzicato* chords, as a rich tonal contrast. The result is one of glossy surface and extrovert colour, but also one of firm control. And this leads to the second general principle: internal balance and functionality. Rimsky's textbook, *Principles of Orchestration*, assembled posthumously from sketches through the generous efforts of Maximilian Steinberg, is an intriguing document of late nineteenth century orchestral craft. Here is the heritage of Berlioz and Meyerbeer, and also something of the tradition of Glinka. There seems to be no doubt what constitutes good orchestration — it is the avoidance of ugly qualities of sound, the balancing of forces so that each instrument has its effect on the texture, and the sensible apportioning of energies. 'One woodwind instrument will balance a section of strings', or 'to double a trumpet in the upper octave, three or four woodwind instruments are required.' There is an air of positivism about it all, of a medium which has grown up with the industrial revolution and acquired the attributes of a mechanism which must function rationally and economically.

The monologue 'My soul is sad' from the coronation scene in the autograph vocal score. It was written before the full score and only the first four scenes survive.

As Rimsky sets out to 'correct' Mussorgsky's orchestration it is in some ways as if a pre-Raphaelite were to 'improve' a Turner seascape: touching up the waves, brightening the palette, making objects clearer. He is concerned to give us an art product which is striking and appealing, but also one which conforms to solid and recognised canons of painterly craft.

No discussion of the orchestration of *Boris* is complete without mention of the bells. They are everywhere in the opera: the coronation, the clock, the funeral bells. The motif seems to have haunted Mussorgsky: at a gathering to mark the funeral of Dostoevsky, not many months before the composer's own death, he improvised a dirge at the piano, which those present recognised as similar to the bells which ring for the death of Boris. There may have been something strangely appropriate in this. It is not surprising that the idea obsessed Mussorgsky; the bell chords are remarkable in a number of ways. They are the harmonic kernel of the opera as a whole: two chords related by a tritone — the 'devil's interval' — the most elusive and intangible interval in the Western tradition; and this interval comes to determine many relationships within the work. The chords themselves are built from conventional intervals, with the addition of a seventh — a note which is regarded as a discord in the grammar of tonal music, seeming to push downwards towards resolution, but one which is also prominent in the natural harmonic series, often audible in bells, and may be accepted as something static and stable. Mussorgsky plays on this ambiguity further by having two notes in common between the two chords, C and F#, which also happen to be a tritone apart. In one chord we hear the F# as a raised F, in the other as a flattened G. The overall effect is to lock the ear in a limbo between resolution and non-resolution, dynamic and static, function and colour. And it is from this terrain of ambiguity that much music of the twentieth century was to grow, above all the music of the French school. It is not inappropriate, therefore, that these pregnant and prophetic sounds should have rung out to mark the death of one who himself anticipated so many things in the philosophy of the century, not least in the West.

There is no doubt that Rimsky's orchestration of the bells is impressive. The

Richard Van Allan in the 1980 ENO production, designed by David Collis. (photo: Reg Wilson)

coronation scene begins with the two common notes, C and F♯, played by bassoons, tuba, harp, piano, and plucked violas, cellos and basses, supported by the tam-tam, in a chilling anticipatory resonance, which continues under the whole passage. The horns and clarinets enter, leaping across their registers to articulate the two chords with maximum contrast, doubled by harp and triangle, and cellos and cymbals, in alternation. Then the 'carillon' effect is introduced in piano and flutes, reinforced by *pizzicato* upper strings. Mussorgsky's version is plain and monochrome by comparison. He chooses to sustain only one of the two common notes — a C in tuba and basses — and the chords are simply divided among the brass. For the 'carillon', however, he throws in his full woodwind and string resources immediately, leaving little headroom for the progressive climax Rimsky is able to muster. There is no doubt as to which version has greater dramatic impact; but what of the aesthetics of the situation, and what were Mussorgsky's real intentions? Rimsky's bells are fairly convincing (although Shostakovich did not think so, and insisted on going one better in his own orchestration), and they seem to narrow the gap between the real bells on stage, and the imitation of bells in the orchestra. Mussorgsky's are much less plausible; but is it not perhaps what he intended? His bells come across as 'icons', musical symbols deliberately abstracted from the objects and sounds they represent, creating a clear distinction between the reality of what is on stage, and the equally autonomous reality of what is music. In Rimsky's version, the rich resonances cloud over the ambiguities of the chord progression, just as they blur the distinction between what is meant to be real and what is meant to be music.

However frequently aesthetics may come to the defence of Mussorgsky's controversial decisions in orchestration, his handling of dramatic form and timing presents special problems. To put it in simple terms, things sometimes seem to end when they clearly should go on, things which appear to be stable seem to change suddenly for no reason, and climaxes may be diffused before they reach their zenith. On the whole, Mussorgsky may appear not be be attuned to most people's idea of how time passes in music drama. A case in point is the Polonaise.

As in the coronation scene, he releases too much volume and too much figurative density too early. Perhaps it has something to do with Mussorgsky's original conception of a string band which gives the impression of a certain uniformity when transplanted to full orchestra, and fails to give a real sense of climax. Rimsky takes a sure line through the material, consistently increasing tension. Mussorgsky's *legato* passages are expunged, *staccato* semiquavers are changed to brisk dotted-note figures. The sweeping woodwind scales and penetrating side-drum accompaniment are held back until a suitable point in the climactic drive. More important still, Mussorgsky cuts the bloom from the rose as soon as it has flowered, bringing the section to a sudden stop as the chorus cheers Marina within the castle. Rimsky keeps Marina on stage a little longer, giving the excuse for a reprise of the Polonaise. In restoring the section to its rightful dance form, Rimsky satisfies not only our musical responses, but also our dramatic anticipation of a closed form — an experience rounded off.

At a closer level, for example in the case of Pimen's monologue in Act One, Rimsky controls and relocates climaxes within individual sections. It is part of a general endeavour to craft a 'melos', and a predictable and eloquent flow of tension and release, where Mussorgsky sometimes brings us to unexpected *crescendos* and sudden hiatuses. At times Rimsky literally papers over cracks. In the same scene, for example, the dialogue between Pimen and Grigory is broken by occasional silences; following his practice in other dialogue scenes, Rimsky prolongs accompanying chords at the beginnings and ends of phrases to cover those lacunae which do not have a palpable dramatic function. He seems to feel a

George Wakewitch's design for Pimen's cell at Covent Garden in 1948. (photo: Donald Southern)

duty to maintain music's role of providing a psychological continuity for music drama: an unbroken thread of orchestral presence.

Mussorgsky, on the other hand, seems happy for his music to fragment, and at times for phrases to drift apart. And the same tendency towards fragmentation is evident even in passages which are otherwise musically continuous and unified. In the second Act, for example, where Shuisky describes the macabre scene at Uglich, there is an imaginative accompaniment, with thirds in contrary motion, which occurs twice. Rimsky seizes a natural opportunity to give this moment a symmetrical frame, simply using the same instrumentation twice — flutes and clarinets with luminous muted string doublings. Mussorgsky, on the other hand, assigns the first statement to wind and the second to strings. It appears that the description of the church is one thing, with bell-like wind, and the description of the corpses, with eerie strings, is another. This all seems to be part of a general tendency for Mussorgsky to live his music moment by moment, sometimes at the expense of continuity, symmetry or formal control. It all has a strange, spontaneous quality; each idea exists as an independent, autonomous entity. There is little sense of reserving resources, as Rimsky carefully marshalls his colours and registers. It is almost tempting to compare it with a fault frequently encountered in early student compositions: to compose rhapsodically, idea by idea, without regard for the functions of cognition and memory which are so important in musical experience. But clearly it is a much more serious and profound matter. If we look at the problem in a broader context and relate this fragmentation of ideas and broken continuities to other facets of style: his dislike of transitions and bridge passages, his tendency to jump *in medias res*, his taste for static, non-progressional harmonies, we may begin to see a pattern. It is the focus of attention on the individual moment, the 'thing-in-itself', an existential quality which anticipates many twentieth century approaches to form. It is, at one extreme, a challenge to German symphonism, something to which Rimsky, for all his Nationalism, was not immune. If we take this view, we may explain many of the problems of formal flow in the work, but we are still unable to explain away the larger-scale problems of dramatic organisation, particularly where a continuous and evolving scenario like *Boris* is concerned; there can be no denying Rimsky's positive contribution in bringing the house to order.

But we may look less positively on his adjustments at the level of phrasing and metre. If, for example, we return to the opening of the opera, we find that Rimsky has not only taken his palette to Mussorgsky's material, but his vice and saw as well. Mussorgsky's beautifully asymmetrical opening phrase — a meandering five-bar melody with a folk-like feel of changing accents, repetition and variation — is moved back half a bar in what appears to be an attempt to give it more conventional melodic direction, and the end of the phrase is chopped off, presumably because of its similarity to the beginning. Similarly in the Hostess's song in Act One scene two, which Mussorgsky bars in an imaginative and elusive combination of three- and four-beat bars, Rimsky drives a simple two-beat wedge through the heart of the melody. Perhaps he is concerned to simplify matters for the orchestra, but in the process he has missed the point of one of Mussorgsky's major contributions: the absorption of features of Russian folk music into serious music, paving the way for the achievements of Stravinsky in works like *Les Noces* some fifty years later. It is reassuring, therefore, that Rimsky leaves Fyodor's marvellous Parrot song in its combination of three- and five-beat bars. Perhaps it is the regular alternation of the two bars and the broader symmetries which result that give him confidence. (By a strange irony, Mussorgsky's first version of the song was barred in four.)

Similarly in the domain of melody and harmony, Rimsky attemps to carpenter Mussorgsky's mystifying radicalism to conform to the canons of nineteenth century musical language. His melodies are shaped by the same primitive forces that control rhythm; they are often modal rather than tonal, and closely related to patterns of folk music and traditional church music. Rimsky sometimes alters notes to make the melodies conform to conventional tonal scales; a simple case occurs at the opening of Act One, where he changes a B♮ in the timelessly winding viola accompaniment to a B♭, changing the scale from Dorian to harmonic minor. Harmonic improprieties worry Rimsky even more. Parallelism is a particular problem. Mussorgsky is fond of taking a chord shape and moving it *en bloc* up and down the piano keyboard, a device which runs contrary to European traditions of harmony, where each strand, or line, is supposed to show independence of movement. In fact, like many of Mussorgsky's devices, it is rooted in the primitive — in this case *organum*, or parallel chanting — but it is also a source of radical renewal, anticipating the parallelism of Debussy and Stravinsky, and the idea of harmony as colour. Rimsky recasts the harmony to give a conventional sense of line and progress, as for example at the end of the second scene of Act One, where Varlaam reads the description of Grishka.

If Rimsky attempts to stem the flow of solecisms, it is eventually an irresistible tide. He may alter cadences, combat sudden key changes by transposing whole sections of the score, he may expunge discords, but in the end, radicalism is a motive force in Mussorgsky's work. Nowhere is melodic and harmonic invention more poignant than in Xenia's lament in Act Two. The haunting Dorian modality of the opening is subtly transformed and modified, then in a sudden modulation, floated over an intimation of the bell chords. The visionary duet between Xenia and Fyodor which ends the passage is a brilliant harmonic inspiration, whose implicit bitonality seems to encapsulate the totality of Debussy's harmonic achievement in a single phrase. Rimsky simply omits the passage; is it because he was concerned about so early an anticipation of the clock? Or could he simply not cope with the shocking inventiveness of Mussorgsky's ear?

These are some of the conflicts of values surrounding the two versions of the opera. If we think of Rimsky's *Boris* striding proudly into the twentieth century, a polished, elegant Boyar, then Mussorgsky's is a humble peasant, stepping hesitantly forward, but carrying hidden beneath his cloak the stratagems of revolt. But if we are concerned with the historical stakes, then we must not underrate the role of Rimsky. Mussorgsky may have given Debussy harmonic inspiration, but it was Rimsky who gave the French school its sensitive ear for timbral focus and brilliance. Mussorgsky may have passed on to Stravinsky the rhythms and paradigms which inspired his work of the Russian period and beyond but it was Rimsky who taught him his craft — the sure template against which new utterances might be forged. If, in *Boris*, Rimsky proved a poor midwife to radicalism, his nursery was a fine school for revolution.

Thematic Guide

Many of the themes from the opera have been identified in the articles by numbers in square brackets, which refer to the themes set out on these pages. The themes are also identified by the numbers in brackets at the corresponding points in the libretto, so that the words can be related to the musical themes.

[1] Andante

[2] Moderato

[3] THE CROWD
Meno mosso

Why for - sake us and leave us help - less great boy - ar?

[4] BOYS
Moderato non troppo lento

Glo - ry to Thee our Lord cre - a - tor of Heav'n and earth!

[5] *The Bells of the Kremlin*
Andantino alla marcia

martellato

[6] THE CROWD
Moderato

Like the sun in the skies su - preme in its glo - ry, glo - ry!

[7] BORIS Meno mosso

My soul is sad

[8] *Pimen*

Andante tranquillo

[9] *Dimitry*

Moderato

pp

[10] **HOSTESS**

Allegretto capriccioso non troppo accelerando

Once I caught a duck, what a stroke of luck

[11] **VARLAAM** *and* **MISSAIL**

Meno mosso

Good Christ - ian peo - ple, du - ti - ful and faith - ful

[12] **VARLAAM** / *The Song of Kazan*

Allegro giusto e con forza

f By the walls of Ka - zan, the mighty fort ress

[13] **VARLAAM**

Andantino mosso

cresc.

He walks a - long, walks all day long,

[14] **XENIA**

Andantino

mf *dimin.*

Where are you, dear - est, where are you be - lov - ed?

[15] **NURSE**

Allegretto scherzando

mf

While the gnat was chopp ing wood and work - ing as good gnats should,

[16] **FYODOR** (*The Clapping Game*)

Più mosso

Here's a song to make peo - ple laugh,

(Andantino) poco meno

Tranquillo

Andante

(Andante)

Andantino molto cantabile

Pol - ly was in our room sit - ting with the nur - ses,

Poco meno mosso

Moderato con grazia, ma semplice

By Vis - la's blue wa - ters, where wil - lows cast sha - dows.

[25] **MARINA**

Moderato non troppo allegro e sempre capriccioso

Oh, these days that pass so slow - ly, days of end - less te - dium,

[26] **RANGONI**

Moderato assai con dolore

been and for -
Our church, a - las has a b - an - doned got - ten

[27] **Meno mosso**

[28] **RANGONI**

(Moderato assai)

words
Lure him with full of am - or - ous pro - mise and words that will rouse him to pas - sion

[29] *Polonaise*

Alla polacca, non troppo allegro

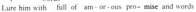

[30] **DIMITRY**

(Moderato) Meno mosso

Ah, how wea - ri - ly, how slow - ly, time seemed to pass as I stood wait - ing

[31] **MARINA**

Più mosso poco a poco, alla polacca capriccioso

your - self
Rise, my tim - id sui - tor do not tire with I - dle plead - ing.

[32] **MARINA**

Andante

words
O Tsa re vich, I im - plore you, do not take to heart the fool - ish that I spoke,

[33]

Andantino molto

[34] **PIMEN**

Moderato

One eve - ning, when all was still there came to me a shepherd

[35] **BORIS**

Moderato

Fare - well, my son, I am dy - ing.

[36]

Allegro non troppo

[37] **CHORUS**

Andantino cantabile

Like a fal - con that's chained in cap - ti - vi - ty

[38] **(Andantino cantabile)**

Ho - nour the great bo - yar, Slave of our wick - ed Tsar

[39] **THE SIMPLETON**

Andantino

Moon - light's shin - ing and kit - ten's whin - ing,

[40] **VARLAAM** *and* **MISSAIL**

Andantino non troppo lento

Dark - ness has swal - lowed sun and moon, —

[41] **THE CROWD**

Vivo

Cast - ing off our chains of bond - age, we shall set our peo - ple free.

Rossi-Lemeni as Boris. (Stuart-Liff Collection)

Boris Godunov

Opera in four acts with a prologue

Music by Modest Mussorgsky
Libretto by the composer, based on Pushkin's
historical tragedy of the same name
and Karamzin's *History of the Russian State*

English translation by David Lloyd-Jones

The opera was first performed (slightly cut) at the Maryinsky Theatre, St Petersburg on January 27, 1874. The first performance outside Russia was in Rimsky-Korsakov's version in Diaghilev's production at the Paris Opéra on May 19, 1908. Toscanini conducted Adamo Didur in the first American production at the Metropolitan on March 19, 1913. The first English performance was during the Russian season at Drury Lane on June 24, 1913, with Chaliapin in Diaghilev's production. The original seven-scene version was heard at Sadler's Wells in English on September 30, 1935.

The transliterated Russian text follows the layout of Mussorgsky's libretto quite closely. Some of his very short lines have been doubled up but the rhythms and rhymes should be perfectly clear.

This translation was first performed by English National Opera in a new production at the London Coliseum on November 26, 1980, which was conducted by David Lloyd-Jones.

The stage directions are an amalgam of many different instructions written by Mussorgsky at different points in the composition: in the libretto, the vocal score and the full score. They have been retained to give as clear an idea as possible of the stage picture. They do not necessarily represent any actual production.

The songs within the text are indicated with capital letters at the beginning of each line. The numbers in square brackets refer to the Thematic Guide.

CHARACTERS

Boris Godunov	*bass*
Fyodor } *his children*	*mezzo-soprano*
Xenia	*soprano*
Xenia's Nurse	*contralto*
Prince Vassily Ivanovich Shuisky	*tenor*
Andrei Shchelkalov *Secretary of the Council of Boyars*	*baritone*
Pimen *a Monk and Chronicler*	*bass*
The Pretender *by name Grigory (a novice in Pimen's care)*	*tenor*
Marina Mniszek *daughter of the Lord of Sandomir*	*mezzo-soprano*
Rangoni *a secret Jesuit*	*bass-baritone*
Varlaam } *vagabonds*	*bass*
Missail	*tenor*
The Hostess of the Inn	*mezzo-soprano*
A Simpleton	*tenor*
Nikitich *a Police Officer*	*bass-baritone*
Mityukha *a peasant*	*baritone*
A Boyar in Attendance	*tenor*
The Boyar Khrushchov	*baritone*
Lavitsky } *Jesuits*	*baritone*
Chernikovsky	*baritone*

Chorus of Boyars, their Children, Streltsy (guards), Soldiers, Police-Officers, Polish Noblemen and Ladies, Sandomir Girls, Wandering Mendicants, the Muscovite People.

Prologue

Scene One. *The courtyard of the Novodievichy monastery near Moscow, surrounded by a wall with turrets. On the right, near the centre of the stage, projects the great gateway of the monastery with its weather-board. When the curtain rises small groups are assembling in front of the monastery walls; they move lazily and their tread is weary. Boyars, headed by Prince Vassily Ivanovich Shuisky, cross the stage and, exchanging greetings with the crowd enter the monastery. When they have left, the crowd begins to wander about.* [1] *Some (chiefly women) peer through the monastery gates; others whisper and scratch their heads. A Police Officer appears at the gates. On seeing him, the crowd collects into one close group and stands motionless, the women resting their cheeks on their hands, the men, hats in hand, with their arms crossed over their belts and their heads bowed.*

POLICE OFFICER
(raising his cudgel, angrily advancing on the motionless crowd) [2]

Wake up there!	Nu, shtozh vy?
Have you frozen into statues?	Shtozh vy idolami stali?
Quickly, on your knees!	Zhivo, na kolyeni!

(The crowd shuffles about.)

Move there!	Nu zhe!

(raising his cudgel)

Come on!	Da nu!

(When the crowd hesitates, he continues impatiently.)

Get to work, you idle rabble!	Eko chortovo otrodye!

(The crowd lazily kneels down.)

THE CROWD
(on its knees, facing the monastery gates) [3]

Why forsake us and leave us helpless, great boyar?	Na kovo ty nas pokidaesh, otyets nash!
Ah, unto whom would you leave your children, kind father?	Akh, na kovo-to ty ostavlyaesh, kormilyets!
Without you we are all orphans, wretched and defenceless.	My, da, vsye tvoi siroty bezzaschchitnyye?
Ah, to you we call, beseeching, weeping, sobbing, praying;	Akh, da, my tebya-to prosim,
See our burning tears!	Molim so slezami, so goryuchimi:

(The Police Officer goes into the monastery.)

Pity us! Pity us! Pity us!	Smiluysya! Smiluysya! Smiluysya!
Boyar, be merciful! Kind father!	Boyarin batyushka! Otyets nash!
Be our guardian!	Ty kormilyets!
Great boyar, pity us!	Boyarin! Smiluysya!

FIRST GROUP OF MEN

Mityukh! Hey, Mityukh, why should we shout?	Mityukh, a Mityukh, chevo oryom?

MITYUKHA

Idiots! Now how would I know?	Vona! pochom ya znayu?

SECOND GROUP OF MEN

A Tsar must be found to govern Russia!	Tsarya na Rusi khotim postavit'!

OLD WOMAN

Oh what a life! I'm hoarse with shouting!	Oy, likhonko! sovsyem okhripla.
Good neighbour, be kind to me,	Golubka, sosyedushka,
and spare a drop of water.	Nye pripasala-l' voditsy?

WOMEN

Well, and who does she think she is?	Vish, boyarynya kakaya!

OTHER WOMEN

She shouted most of all and now she says she's thirsty!	Orala pushche vsyekh, Sama-b i pripasala.

A MAN

Now then, women, stop your cackle!	Nu vy, baby, nye gutorit'!

OLD WOMEN

Who are you to give us orders?	A ty shto za ukaschik!

MAN

Quiet!	Nishkni!

OLD WOMEN

His Lordship's asked for silence!	Vish, pristav navyazalsya!

MITYUKHA

Hey, you witches, stop that racket!	Oy, vy, vyed'my nye bushuyte!

THE CROWD
(women, bad temperedly)

Oh, confound the ugly rascal!	Akh, postryel ty okayanny!
Isn't he the very devil?	Vot-to nyekhrist otyskalsya!
He's a vile and wicked heathen!	Eko dyavol privyazalsya!
Lord forgive his evil slander!	Prosti, gospodi, besstydnik!
Come along we'd best be going.	Oy uydyomte luchshe, baby,
Why should we endure such language?	Ot byedy, da ot napasti.
That's as much as we are taking!	Ot byedi uyti podal'she.
This is far too hard and trying,	Podobru, da pozdorovu!
Let's go home, it will be wiser!	Ved'my vput' uzh sobralisya.

(men, laughing)

You don't seem to like the nickname.	Nye ponravilasya klichka
If the cap fits you can wear it.	Vidno solno prishlasya,
That's a good one, did it sting you?	Nye v ugodu, nye po vkusu.
Mind you don't forget your broomsticks!	Vedmy vput' uzh sobralisya.
Ha, ha, ha!	Kho, kho, kho!

They rise, preparing to leave. The Police Officer appears at the monastery gate. Seeing him, the women quickly kneel down. All remain motionless as before.

POLICE OFFICER
(to the crowd) [2]

What's this? Still silent? You're resting are you?	Shtozh vy? shtozh smolkli? Al' glotok zhalko?

(raising his cudgel)

I'll teach you! Maybe all you need's a whipping to remind you!	Vot ya vas! Al' davno po spinam plyotka nye gulyala!

(advancing on the crowd)

Right, I'll show you this minute!	Prouchu vas . . . ya zhivo!

WOMEN
(kneeling)

Don't be cross, Mikitich, give us just a moment!	Nye serchay, Mikitich, Nye serchay, rodimy!

MEN
(kneeling)

Once we've got our breath back, then we'll shout much louder.	Tol'ko pootdokhnyem, Zaoryom my snova.

THE CROWD
(men and women)

Can't we breathe a while, you devil!	I vzdokhnut' nye dast, proklyaty.

Come on!	Nu-ka!
Shout as loudly as you can!	Tol'ko glotok nye zhalyet'!

THE CROWD

Right then.	Ladno!

POLICE OFFICER
(*raising his cudgel*)

Shout!	Nu?

THE CROWD
(*plaintively*) [3]

Why forsake us and leave us helpless, great boyar?	Na kovo ty nas pokidaesh, otyets nash!
Unto whom would you leave your children, kind father!	Na kovo-to ty ostavlyaesh, rodimy!
Without you we are orphans.	My tebya, siroty, prosim,
Hear us weeping, sobbing, praying; see our burning tears.	Molim so slezami, so goryuchimi:
Pity us! Pity us!	Smiluysya! Smiluysya!

(*The Police Officer threatens them again.*)

Boyar, be merciful!	Boyarin batyushka!
Kind father! Kind father!	Otyets nash! Otyets nash!
Great boyar! Ah!	Kormilyets! Kormilyets! A-a-a!

During the last bars, the secretary of the Duma, Shchelkalov, has appeared at the monastery gateway.

POLICE OFFICER
(*Seeing him, he makes a sign to the people and hurries towards them.*)

Silence! Get up there!	Nishkni! Vstavayete!

(*The people rise.*)

News from the boyars' council.	Dyak dumny govorit.

SHCHELKALOV
(*He descends the steps slowly and pensively, coming towards the crowd. He takes off his hat and bows deeply.*)

O my countrymen: Boris rejects our pleading!	Pravoslavnyye! nye umolim boyarin!
In vain the Church and holy council have tried to move him,	Na skorbny zov Boyarskoy Dumy i Patriakha,
but still he won't accept the throne of Russia.	I slyshat' nye khotyel o tronye tsarskom.
Disaster has come, disaster for all of us, O my countrymen!	Pechal' na Rusi . . . pechal' bezyskhodnaya, Pravoslavnyye!
Russia is doomed: who can save her?	Stonyet zemlya v zlom bespravyi.
So pray to the Lord God in Heaven and ask for mercy,	Ko gospodu sil pripadite.
beg him to spare Holy Russia,	Da nishposhlyot on
and to Boris send heavenly wisdom	Skorbnoy Rusi uteshenye . . .
to strengthen his weary soul.	I ozarit nebyesnym svyetom Borisa ustaly dukh!

He goes back into the monastery. The people are perplexed. The singing of blind pilgrims is heard off stage. The scene is lit by the reddish glow of the setting sun. The crowd listens to the distant singing.

LEADERS OF THE BLIND PILGRIMS
(*boys, off-stage*) [4]

Glory to Thee our Lord, creator of Heaven and Earth,	Slava tebye, tvortsu vsevyshnemu, na zemli,
Blessed be Thy Holy Name in Heaven above,	Slava silam tvoim nebyesnym,
To saints and angels glory in our land.	I vsyem ugodnikam, Slava na Rusi!

PILGRIMS
(*off-stage*) [4]

Glory to Thee Almighty God, Glory!	Slava tebye vsevyshnemu, Slava!

THE CROWD
(*whispering*)

Holy pilgrims!	Bozhyi lyudi!

PILGRIMS
(*coming nearer*)

Thus spake the Angel of the Lord:	Angel gospoden miru rek:
Rise, ye stormclouds,	Podnimaytes tuchi groznyye.
over Russia's land,	Nesites na zemlyu russkuyu!
bringing fright and terror in your wake,	Vy nesites po podnebyesyu,
rise, ye stormclouds over this sinful land!	Zastilayte zemlyu russkuyu!

They enter: first the leaders, then, leaning on their shoulders, the pilgrims with hoods and hung with holy images and amulets, and holding staffs. The crowd salutes them respectfully and devoutly, and makes way for them.

LEADERS AND PILGRIMS

Crush the fearful serpent, crush the fierce,	Sokrushite zmiya lyuta
twelve-winged, rampant monster who fouls the earth,	So dvanadesyatyu krylami khoboty.
breeder of dissension, sowing discord in our Tsarless land.	Tavo zmiya, smutu russkuyu, da beznachaliye.
And to Russians who are Orthodox may salvation come!	Vozvestite pravoslavniim da vo spasenye!

(*They distribute images and amulets among the crowd.*)

Don ye all your festal robes of white,	Oblekaytes v rizy svyetlyye,
take the image of Mary, Our Lady,	Podnimayte ikony vladychitsy.
bring forth the ikons of our guardian Saints,	I so Donskoy, i so Vladimirskoy.
and go to acclaim your Tsar straight way!	Gryadite tsaryu vo sretenye!

(*They leave, making their way into the monastery.*)

Sing hymns to God our Lord,	Vospoyte slavu bozhyu,
praising his angels and the Saints on high!	Slavu sil svyatykh nebyesnykh!

(*off-stage, gradually fainter*)

Glory to Thee, Lord God, on this earth!	Slava tebye, tvortsu, na zemli!
Praise the Lord who in Heaven reigns!	Slava ottsu nebyesnomu!

They disappear into the monastery. Some of the people compare with each other the images and amulets they have received. Others, from the foreground, watch the pilgrims leave.

PART OF THE CROWD
(*to Mityukha*)

Mityukh, what were the holy pilgrims saying?	Slykhal, shto bozhyi lyudi govorili?

MITYUKHA

They said:	Slykhal!
Bring forth the ikons of our guardian Saints ...	I so Donskoy, i so Vladimirskoy ...

(*forgetting*)

PART OF THE CROWD

Well?	Nu!

(*The women start squabbling about the amulets.*)

MITYUKHA
(*struggling to remember*)

Bring forth the ikons of our guardian Saints and pay homage ...	I so Donskoy, i so Vladimirskoy ... Vy idite ...

PART OF THE CROWD

To whom?	Chevo?

MITYUKHA
(*thoughtfully*)

... pay homage ...	... idite ...

PART OF THE CROWD

Well?   Nu!

MITYUKHA
(*losing patience*)

... guardian Saints pay homage ...   ... So Donskoy, idite ...

(*He gives up trying to remember and turns away.*)

PART OF THE CROWD
(*pointing to him*)

Nonsense!   Plokh, brat!

ANOTHER PART OF THE CROWD
(*coming closer*)

Don ye all your festal robes of white.   Oblekaytes v rizy svyetlyye.
Bring forth the ikons of our guardian Saints,   I so Donskoy, i so Vladimirskoy
and go forth to acclaim your Tsar straight-   Vy gryadite k tsaryu vo sretenye.
way.

PART OF THE CROWD

Our Tsar? But who is our Tsar?   Tsaryu? Kakomu tsaryu?

POLICE OFFICER
(*coming out of the monastery into which he had escorted the pilgrims*)

Hey,there!   Ey, vy!

ANOTHER PART OF THE CROWD
(*not noticing the Police Officer*)

Can't you guess?   Kak kakomu?
It's Boris!   A Borisu ...

POLICE OFFICER
(*coming towards them*)

Listen, you pack of half-wits! Are you deaf?   Ey, vy, baranye stado! Al' oglokhli!

(*The crowd clusters together.*)

These are your new instructions: Vam ot boyar ukaz:
Go over to the Kremlin   Zautra byt' v Kremlye
and wait for further orders.   I zhdat' tam prikazaniy.
Off with you!   Slyshali?

(*Exit.*)

(*Darkness falls, the crowd begins to disperse.*)

THE CROWD

Ah well! They've got to keep us busy!   Vona! za dyelom sobirali!
The Kremlin is it?   A nam-to shto?
If we must shout it might as well be there.   Velyat zavyt', zavoyem i v kremlye!
Who cares! All the same to us!   Zavoyem. Dlya cha nye zavyt'
Right, let's go, you fellows!   Shtozh? Idyom, rebyata!

The stage gradually empties.

Curtain.

Scene Two. *A square in the Moscow Kremlin. Facing the audience, up stage, the Great staircase of the Imperial Palace. Right, down stage, the crowd is kneeling in the space between the Cathedral of the Assumption (right) and the Cathedral of the Archangels (left, up stage). The porches of both Cathedrals can be seen. Solemn peals of bells. Loud chimes on stage. From the Great Staircase boyars in solemn procession begin to move towards the Cathedral of the Assumption; in front are guards, Streltsy, and the children of the boyars; then comes Shuisky, carrying the crown of Monomach on a cushion. Behind him, more boyars and Shchelkalov carrying the Imperial sceptre; then more Streltsy, the chief boyars, the secretaries, etc.. The procession passes through the crowd and enters the Cathedral of the Assumption. The Streltsy stand in rows on both sides of the steps. The chimes on stage continue.* [5]

(appearing in the porch of the Cathedral of the Assumption; to the crowd)

Long life to our Tsar Boris Fyodorovich!   Da zdravstvuet tsar Boris Fyodorovich!

(The crowd stands up.)

THE CROWD

Long live our sovereign, Tsar of Russia!   Zhivi i zdravstvuy, tsar nash batyushka!

SHUISKY

Hail him!   Slav'te!
(He re-enters the Cathedral.)

THE CROWD

Like the sun in the skies, supreme in its [6] Uzh kak na nyebye solntsu krasnomu,
    glory,   Slava, Slava!
Over Russia our Tsar Boris now reigns in   Uzh i kak na Rusi tsaryu Borisu Slava,
    glory!   Slava!

(The Tsar's procession comes out of the Cathedral of the Assumption. The police officers marshal the people into rows.)

Long live our sovereign!   Zhivi i zdravstvuy! Zhivi i zdravstvuy!
Tsar, our guardian!   Tsar nash batyushka!

(Trumpeters take places facing the audience, in front of the crowd.)

Raise your voices, people!   Raduysya lyud!
Now exult and be joyful, people!   Raduysya, veselisya lyud!
Faithful Christian people!   Pravoslavny lyud!
Let all hail our Tsar Boris, and rejoice!   Velichay tsarya Borisa i slav!

BOYARS
(from the Cathedral porch, to the crowd)

All hail to thee, Tsar Boris Fyodorovich!   Da zdravstvuet tsar Boris Fyodorovich!
(They come down the steps.)

THE CROWD
(bowing deeply to the boyars)

All hail to thee!   Da zdravstvuet!

(Shchelkalov and the boyars follow the procession, and form a semi-circle extending from the Cathedral of the Archangels to the Cathedral of the Assumption.)

Over Russia Boris now reigns in glory,   Uzh kak na Rusi tsaryu Borisu Slava,
reigns in glory! Glory! Glory!   Slava tsaryu, Slava! Slava!

Boris appears in the Cathedral porch. Shuisky, behind the Tsar's back, signals to the people to keep silence, and with Vorotynsky takes his place behind Boris. The chimes cease.

BORIS
(From the porch; his children, Fyodor and Xenia, are behind him.)

My soul is sad!   [7] Skorbit dusha!
A secret terror haunts me;   Kakoy-to strakh nevol'ny
with evil presentiments my heart is stifled.   Zlovyeshchim predchuvstviem skoval
                         mnye syerdtse.
(in a mood of exaltation)

O Lord above! O Thou Almighty Father!   O, pravednik, o moy otyets derzhavny!
From Heaven's throne behold my contrite   Vozri s nebyes na slyozy vyernykh slug
    tears,
and with Thy blessing grant me holiness   I nisposhli to mnye svyshchennoye
and strength, that they may guide me.   Na vlast blagoslovyenye:
(with humility)

O make me just and merciful as Thou;   Da budu blag i praveden kak ty.
in glory let me rule my land.   Da v slavye pravlyu svoy narod.
(He bows his head in prayer. Then, raising his head, sternly)

Now let us kneel and pay our homage   Tepyer poklonimsa
at the tombs of Russia's monarchs.   Pochiyushchim vlastitelyam Rusii,

(majestically)

And then our people all shall feast,
yea, every man, from boyar down to serf;
all shall we greet, all gladly shall we
welcome!

A tam szyvat' narod na pir,
Vsyekh, ot boyar do nishchevo slepts-a:
Vsyem vol'ny vkhod, vsye gosti dorogiye.

(Bells on stage. Boris, accompanied by Shuisky and Vorotinky, comes down the steps. The boyars and Streltsy follow. The procession proceeds towards the Cathedral of the Archangels.)

THE CROWD

Glory, glory, glory!
Long live our sovereign, Tsar of Russia!

Slava, Slava, Slava!
Zhivi i zdravstvuy, tsar nash batyushka!

(The people rush towards the Cathedral. The police maintain order.)

Honour and glory to you our father!
As the sun shines supreme in its glory,
over Russia Boris now reigns in glory,
and long may he prosper!

[6] Mnogaya lyeta tsaryu Borisu!
Uzh kak na nyebye solnyshku, Slava!
Uzh kak na Rusi tsaryu Borisu, Slava!
Slava i mnogaya lyeta!

(Tumult. The police struggle with the crowd. Boris comes out of the Cathedral of the Archangels and proceeds towards the palace.)

Glory, glory, glory!

Slava, Slava, Slava!

Curtain.

George Wakewitch's design for the coronation scene at Covent Garden in 1948. (Covent Garden Archives)

Act One

Scene One. *Night. A cell in the Chudov Monastery. Pimen is writing by lamplight. Grigory is asleep.*

PIMEN
(He stops writing.)

Just one more tale. The final chapter opens,	Yeshcho odno poslyedneye skazanye
my work will be completed then at last;	I lyetopis okonchena moya.
complete the task assigned by God Almighty	Okonchen trud, zaveshchany ot Boga
to me, sinful one.	Mnye gryeshnomu.

(He resumes his writing, then stops.)

And not in vain has God	Nedarom mnogikh lyet
appointed me to serve him as his witness.	Svidyetelem Gospod' menya postavil.
In days to come another of our order	Kogda-nibud' monakh trudolyubivy
will find my work, my careful, nameless story;	Naydyot moy trud usyerdny, bezymyany;
and late at night, like me, he'll light his candle	Zasvyetit on, kak ya, svoyu lampadu
and shake the dust of ages from the scroll,	I, pyl vekov ot kharty otryakhnuv,
then piously transcribe what I have written,	Pravdivyye skazanya perepishet:
so future generations of the faithful	Da vyedayut potomki pravoslavnykh
will come to learn the history of their past.	Zemli rodnoy minuvshuyu sud'bu.

(lost in thought)

It seems that I relive these bygone times;	Na starosti ya syznova zhivu;
Those former years of turmoil pass before [8] me,	Minuvsheye prokhodit predo mnoyu,
tempestuous as the sea in times of storm.	Volnuyasa kak morye okian . . .
They once appeared so wild, so loud with clamour.	Davnol' ono neslos sobytiy polno?
But now they pass serenely and in silence.	Tepyer ono spokoyno i bezmolvno! . . .
But now the dawn is near . . . my candle flickers feebly . . .	Odnako blizok dyen . . . Lampada dogorayet . . .

(He writes.)

Just one more tale: the final chapter opens.	Yeshcho odno poslyedneye skazanye.

(He continues to write.)

MONKS
(off-stage)

Lord, our Heavenly Father,	Bozhe krepky, pravy,
have mercy on Thy slaves.	Vnemli rabam tvoim,
Hear as we cry!	Molyashchim tya!
Lead us not into temptation	Dukh lzhemudriya lukavy
but delivery us from harm,	Otzheni ot chad tvoikh
grant us Thy peace!	Veryashchik ti!

GRIGORY
(waking)

Always that dream!	Vsyo tot zhe son!
Yet again: once more that dream!	V tretiy raz vsyo tot zhe son!
How it haunts me! Accursed dream!	Neotvyazny, proklyaty son . . .
All the while he sits there writing, and he's weary —	A starik sidit, da pishet, i dremotoy
that means all night he never closed his eyes.	Znat', vo vsyu noch on nye smykal ochey.
Ah, how benign he looks, how wise and mild.	Kak ya lyublyu yevo smirenny vid,
I love to watch as, lost in meditation,	Kogda, dushoy v minuvshem pogruzhonny,
he sits there at his writing, so dignified and calm . . .	Spokoyny, velichavy, on lyetopis svoyu . . .

Awake, my son?   Prosnulsya, brat?

GRIGORY
(*He goes up to Pimen and bows deeply.*)

Grant me your blessing, most holy father.   Blagoslovi menya, chestnoy otyets.

MONKS
(*off-stage*)

Why, O Lord, my God,   Bozhe, Bozhe moy
hast Thou forsaken me?   Vskuyu ostavil mya!

PIMEN
(*He rises and blesses him.*)

The grace of God on high be thine,   Blagoslovi tebya gospod',
today, from henceforth and for ever.   I dnyes, i prisno, i vo vyeki.
(*He sits down.*)

GRIGORY
(*rising*)

You have not slept — all night you have   Ty vsyo pisal i snom nye pozabylsya:
  been writing;
while my repose was filled with evil visions;   A moy pokoy besovskoye mechtanye
the devil came to mock me in my sleep.   Trevozhilo, i vrag menya mutil.
I dreamt that climbing up a stairway   Mnye snilos: lyesnitsa krutaya vela
I reached a lofty tower; from the top   Vela menya na bashnyu; s vysoty
I saw before me Moscow. Just like an anthill   Mnye videlas Moskva, shto muravyeynik;
the crowd, it seemed, were swarming down   Narod vnizu na ploshchadi kipyel
  below
and pointing up, they mocked me with   I na menya ukazyval so smyekhom . . .
  their laughter . . .
What shame I felt, what terror overcame   I stydno mnye, i strashno stanovilos . . .
  me . . .
Then suddenly I fell, and so awakened.   I, padaya stremglav, ya probuzhdalsya.

PIMEN

Your youthful blood is stirring!   Mladaya krov igraet;
Subdue yourself with fasting and with   Smiryay sebya molitvoy i postom.
  prayer,
and peace will then be yours in sleeping and   I sny tvoi videniy lyokhkikh budut polny.
  in dreaming.
Believe me, even if I,   Donyne, yesli ya
when sometimes overcome by sudden   Nevolnoyu dremotoy obessilyen,
  tiredness,
have fallen asleep before I've said my   Nye sotvoryu molitvy dolgoy k nochi,
  prayers,
my soul can find no peace, my dreams are   Moy stary son nye tikh i nye bezgreshen:
  sinful,
for visions rise of wild and wanton feasts,   Mnye chudyatsa to buynye piry.
of skirmishes and battles;   To skhvatki boevyye:
vain pleasures and pursuits of wayward   Bezumnyye potyekhi yunykh lyet!
  youth!

GRIGORY

How joyfully you spent your years of   Kak vyeselo provyol ty svoyu mladost'!
  boyhood!
You went to war, and fought in Lithuania;   Ty voeval pod bashnyami Kazani,
you helped to storm the fortress of Kazan;   Ty rat' Litvy pri Shuyskom otrazhal,
you saw Ivan, his court and all its splendour!   Ty videl dvor i roskosh Ioanna!
Yet I have whiled away my youth   A ya ot otrocheskikh lyet
in cloisters and in cells, a wretched novice.   Po kyeliyam skitayus, byedny inok!
Why cannot I enjoy the thrill of war,   Zachem i mnye nye tyeshit'sya v boyakh,
and take my seat with Tsars at royal   Nye pirovat' za tsarskoyu trapezoy?
  banquets?

PIMEN
(He restrains Grigory by the arm.)

Don't grieve that you renounced the world
   of sin so early. Mark my words:
we're far removed from idle pleasure
and woman's subtle blandishments of love.
Just think, my son, about the Tsars of
   Russia.
They ruled supreme; yet often,
Oh how gladly, gladly, they would have
given their royal sceptre and their purple,
renouncing pomp and splendour,
to wear a humble robe of sackcloth
and find the peace of God within a holy
   cloister.
Here, in this very cell,
(it then belonged to Kyril, the blessed
   hermit,
that righteous man), here I have seen the
   Tsar.
Reflective, sad, sat Tsar Ivan the Terrible.
And from his lips flowed words of deep
   remorse,
while from his eyes so full of sternness,
in penitence the tears were falling.
He wept before us . . .

Nye syetuy, brat, shto rano greshny svyet
   pokinul. Ver ty mnye:
Nas izdali plenyaet roskosh
I zhenskaya lukavaya lyubov.
Pomysli, syn, ty o tsaryakh velikikh.

Kto vyshe ikh? i shto-zhe:
O kak chasto, chasto oni menyali
Svoy posokh tsarsky, i profiru,
I svoy venyets roskoshny,
Na inokov klobuk smirenny,
I v kyelii svyatoy dushoyu otdykhali . . .

Zdyes, v etoy samoy kyelye,
(V ney zhil togda Kirill mnogostradal'ny

muzh pravyedny), zdyes videl ya tsarya.

Zadumchiv, tikh sidyel pred nami Grozny;
I tikho rech iz ust yevo lilasya,

A v ochakh yevo surovykh
Raskayanya sleza drozhala . . .
I plakal on . . .

(He becomes thoughtful.)

His son, the Tsar Fyodor, transformed the
   royal palace
into a house of prayer and meditation.
God favoured well such meekness from a
   Tsar
and Russia in his time was free from
   turmoil and
prosperous. And in his dying hour
an awe-inspiring miracle was witnessed.
His palace was filled with sweet and
   heavenly fragrance.
His visage shone as radiant as the sun.
We shall not see a Tsar like that again:
we've angered God Almighty, we are
   sinners,
and now we must endure a cursed regicide
   as Tsar!

A syn yevo Feodor? On tsarskiye chertogi

Preobratil v molitvennuyu kyel'yu;
Bog vozlyubil smiryeniye tsarya,

I Rus pri nyom, vo slave bezmyatezhnoy

Uteshilas. A v chas yevo konchiny,
Svershilosa neslykhannoye chudo:
Palaty ispolnilis blagoukhanyem . . .

I lik yevo kak solntse prosiyal! . . .
Uzh nye vidat' takovo nam tsarya!
Prognevali my Boga, sogreshili:

Sogreshili: vladykoyu sebye tsareubiytsy
   narekli!

GRIGORY

For long now, my holy father,
I've meant to ask you to recall the death
of Dimitry the Tsarevich.
Did you not live in Uglich, and witness
   the deed?

Davno, chestnoy otyets,
Khotyelos mnye tebya sprosit' o smyerti
Dimitriya tsaryevicha.
Ty, govoryat, v to vremya byl v Ugliche?

(During the following narrative, Grigory goes to sit at the table and listens with rapt attention.)

PIMEN

Yes truly!
The Lord ordained that I
should see the crime committed; that
   bloody deed!
I had at that time been
sent to distant Uglich as a penance.
I came at night . . . Next morning . . . after
   matins . . .
all heard a bell, it sounded the alarm;
cries, shouts; a rush towards the palace . . .

Okh pomnyu!
Privyol menya gospod'
Uvidet' zloye dyelo, krovavy grekh.

Togda ya v Uglich
Na nyekoe byl uslan poslushanye.
Prishol ya v noch . . . na utro v chas
   obyedni
Vdrug slyshu zvon; udarili v nabat;
Krik, shum. Begut vo dvor tsaritsy . . .

I went too, and saw:	Ya tudazh, glyazhu:
all steeped in blood the murdered infant lay there;	Lezhit v krovi zarezanny tsaryevich;
close by his side his mother lay unconscious,	Tsaritsa mat' v bezpamyatstve nad nim,
and near to her the nurse who once had suckled him	Kormilitsa neschastnaya v otchayani
was sobbing. Outside, the crowd were	Rydaet. A tam, na ploshchadi
growing frenzied in their grief,	Narod ostervenyas volochit
and dragged out the woman who'd betrayed the dead Tsarevich ...	Bezbozhnuyu predatel'nitsu mamku ...
Sobs! ... Curses! ...	Vopl'! ... Stony! ...
Then all at once, aghast and pale with hatred, among them	Vdrug mezhdu nikh, sivryep, Ot zlosti blyeden,
stood the Judas Bityagovsky ...	Yavlyaetsya Iuda Bityagovskiy ...
'That's him, there, that's the man!'	'Vot on, vot, vot zlodyey!'
arose the common cry.	Razdal'sa obshchiy vopl'.
He escaped, followed by the crowd	Tut narod brosilsa vo sled
who chased the fleeing murderers.	Bezhavshim tryom ubiytsam.
The villain soon was captured;	Zlodyeyev zakhvatili i priveli
and then was brought to view the dead Tsarevich ...	Pryed tyoply trup mladentsa ...
Oh wonder! For the corpse began to tremble ...	I chudo! Vdrug mertvyets zatrepetal ...
'Confess the crime!', the people cried aloud:	'Pokaytesya!' narod im zagremyel.
and terrified, beneath the axe,	I v uzhase pod toporom
the murderer confessed the deed	Zlodyei pokayalis,
and swore Boris had planned it ...	I nazvali Borisa.

GRIGORY

And when he died how old was the Tsarevich?	Kakikh byl lyet tsaryevich ubiyenny?

PIMEN
(*remembering*)

He was seven. But wait!	Lyet semi. Postoy!
Have ten years passed already?	S tyekh por proshlo lyet dyesyat'?
Can it be? Or twelve years?	Ili nyet! Dvenadsat'?
Yes, yes, it is twelve years.	Da, tak: dvenadsat' lyet.
He'd be as old as you are,	On byl by tvoy rovyesnik
and Tsar today!	I tsarstvoval!

(*At this point Grigory rises, majestic, head high, then with feigned humility, sits down again.*)

But God did not ordain it.	No Bog sudil inoye.
The crime to which Boris now owes his kingdom will conclude	Borisa prestuplyenyem vopiyushchim zaklyuchu
this chronicle of mine. Son Grigory!	Ya lyetopis svoyu. Brat Grigoriy!
Already you have learnt to read and write	Ty gramotoy svoy razum prosvetil,
and soon I'll leave my work to you.	Tebye moy trud peredayu ...
Record in full, avoiding guile and malice,	Opisivay, nye mudrstvuya lukavo,
everything you witness in your lifetime —	Vsyo, chemu svidyetel' v zhizni budyesh:
be it war or peace, the government of monarchs,	Voynu il' mir, upravu gosudarey,
all prophecies and miracles from Heaven ...	Prorochestva i znamenya nebyesny ...
But as for me, the time has come to rest.	A mnye pora, pora uzh otdokhnut' ...

(*He rises and puts out his lamp. The distant monastery bell is heard ringing off-stage. He listens.*)

The bell ... it's matins time.	Zvonyat k zautrenye ...

(*He puts on his monk's cap.*)

Bestow Thy blessing, Lord, upon Thy slaves!	Blagoslovi, gospod', svoikh rabov!
Pray pass my staff, Grigory!	Poday kostyl', Grigory!

MONKS
(*off-stage*)

Have mercy upon us,	Pomiluy nas, bozhe,
have mercy, Lord, save us all ...	Pomiluy nas, vsyeblagy!
Father, our blessed Saviour,	Otche nash, vsederzhitel',

| God of truth and justice, | Bozhe vyechny, pravy, |
| have mercy, Lord! | Pomiluy nas! |

Pimen walks away, head bent in prayer. Grigory follows him, but remains standing by the door.

GRIGORY
(*by the door*)

Boris, Boris! All stand in awe before you,	Boris, Boris, vsye pryed toboy trepyeshchet,
and none will ever dare to mention	Nikto nye smyeyet i napomnit'
the murder of the innocent Tsarevich.	O zhrebiy neschastnovo mladentsa.

(*He goes to the table.*)

But all the while a humble monk condemns you:	A mezhdu tyem otshel'nik v tyomnoy kyelye
here in this cell your hellish crime is noted,	Zdyes na tebya donos uzhasny pishet;
and you will have to face the people's judgement,	I nye uydyosh ty ot suda lyudskovo,
as you will face the God who is your judge . . .	Kak nye uydyosh ot bozhevo suda . . .

(*Exit.*)

Curtain.

Scene Two. *An Inn near the Lithuanian border. To the audience's right, a door leading into the pantry. Facing the audience, the entrance door. Slightly to left of it, a window.* [12, 11, 9]

THE HOSTESS
(*She sits darning an old bodice.*) [10]

Once I caught a duck — what a stroke of luck!	Poymala ya siza seleznya,
Ah, duckling don't be coy,	Okh, ty, moy syelezen,
come to me my lovely boy!	Moy kasatik, syelezen.
You shall have your nest when you need a rest —	Posazhu tebya, siza seleznya,
Somewhere nice beside a pool,	Okh, na chistenkiy prudok,
where the shade is deep and cool.	Pod rakitovy kustok.
Flap your wings and fly,	Ty porkhni, porkhni,
frolic in the sky!	Sizy syelezen,
Though I have to set you free,	Oy, vzvyeysa, podnimis,
you will soon come back to me!	K byednenkoy ko mnye spustis.
In your nest so snug, you and I will hug.	Polyublyu tebya, prigolublyu ya,
Charm me with your eyes so bright!	Mavo milova druzhka,
kiss me once and hold me tight!	Kasatika syeleznya!
Come and sit by me,	Ty prisyad' ko mnye,

(*Off-stage, the sound of travellers talking in the distance.*)

close as close can be.	Da poblizhe,
Darling duckling green and grey,	Oboymi menya, druzhok,
help me pass the time away.	Potsaluy menya razok.

(*Off-stage talking and coarse laughter. Hostess listens.*)

| What was that? | Evona! |

(*The talking becomes louder.*)

| Some passers-by . . . | Prokhozhiy lyud . . . |
| Customers who're thirsty! | Gosti dorogie! |

(*Silence off-stage*)

But no . . . no one!	Au! Smolkli! . . .
They've passed me without stopping!	Znat' mimo promakhnuli . . .
Kiss and kiss again, make it linger!	Rastsaluy menya, da po zharche,
Ah, duckling, don't be coy, kiss again my lovely boy.	Okh, ty, moy syelezen,
Comfort me, yes, comfort me a lonely widow,	Ty potyesh menya, potyesh menya vdovuy,
Lonely widow bent on joy . . .	Vdovushku vol'nuyu . . .

(*outside the door*) [11]

Good Christian people,	Lyud khristiansky,
dutiful and faithful,	Lyud chestnoy, gospodniy,
spare a little offering	Na stroyenye khramov
to build another monastery.	Pozhertvuy khot' kopyeyechku,
Ample will be your reward in Heaven!	Lyepta vozdastsa tebye storitsey.

HOSTESS
(*listening, greatly perturbed*)

Goodness gracious, some friars are coming!	Akh, ty, gospodi, startsy chestnyye!
Oh, I'm a stupid old chatter-box,	Dura ya, dura okol'naya,
quite unprepared for visitors!	Staraya grekhovodnitsa!

(*going to the window*)

Yes, indeed!	Tak i yest'! . . .

(*walking to and fro*)

I'm right . . . Two holy fathers . . .	Oni . . . chestnyye startsy . . .

She goes to the door and opens it. Enter Varlaam and Missail, followed by Grigory (now the pretender-to-be, the false Dimitry) in peasants' clothes. The Hostess curtseys deeply and with reverence.

VARLAAM

Good woman, greetings; peace unto this house!	Zheno, mir domu tvoemu!

HOSTESS
(*curtseying again*)

Say what I may offer you,	Chem-to mnye vas podchivat',
reverend fathers?	Startsy chestnyye?

MISSAIL
(*humbly*)

Oh, anything that God provides!	Chem bog poslal, khozyayushka.

VARLAAM
(*nudging Missail*)

Have you no wine?	Nyet li vina?

HOSTESS
(*quickly*)

Why, of course, your reverence!	Kak nye byt', otsy moi!
Just wait, I'll fetch you some.	Seychas vynesu.

She goes out into the pantry. [10] *Varlaam watches Grigory, who is sitting by the table, lost in thought.*

VARLAAM
(*going to Grigory*)

Why are you so miserable, young fellow?	Shtozh ty prizadumalsa, tovarishch?
Here now at last is the border, Lithuania,	Viot i granitsa litovskaya,
the country you're anxious to get to.	Do kotoroy tebye tak khotyelos dobrat'sya.

GRIGORY
(*at the table, moodily*)

I shall not feel at my ease	Poka nye budu v Litvye,
till I'm over the border.	Nye mogu byt' spokoen.

VARLAAM

But why is Lithuania so special?	Da, shto tebye Litva tak slyubilas!
Take us, the good Missail and I,	Vot my, otyets Misail,
wretched sinner,	Da az mnogogreshny,
since we slipped out slyly from our cells	Kat utekli iz monastyrya,
all is one as far as we care;	Tak i v us sebye nye duem!
it may be Russia,	Litva li, Rus li,
Lithuania, Prussia —	Shto gudok, shto gusli,

anywhere's fine	Vsyo nam ravno,
where there is wine!	Bylo b vino!

Re-enter Hostess, carrying some bottles. [10] *Varlaam continues merrily, as he sees the Hostess.*

It's come in good time!	Da vot i ono!

HOSTESS
(putting the bottles on the table)

There, now, my reverend sirs,	Vot vam, otsy moi,
May you both enjoy it!	Pyeyte na zdorovye.

MISSAIL AND VARLAAM

We thank you, good hostess,	Spasibo, khozyayushka,
and God will give you recompense!	Bog tebya blagoslovi!

(They fill their glasses and drink. Grigory refrains from joining them.)

VARLAAM
(bottle in hand) [12]

By the walls of Kazan the mighty fortress,	Kak vo gorode bylo vo Kazane,
Tsar Ivan made a celebrated conquest.	Grozny Tsar piroval, da veselilsa.
There the Tartars took a beating,	On tatarey bil neshchadno,
There began their long retreating.	Shtob im bylo nepovadno,
Russia was free once more!	Vdol' po Rusi gulyat'.

(He drinks.)

Tsar Ivan advanced his army to the town of Kazan:	Tsar podkhodom podkhodil, Da, pod Kazan gorodok,
There he tunnelled out a trench beneath the broad river bed.	On podkopy podkopal, da, pod Kazanku reku.
All the time the wicked Tartars felt as safe as before.	Kak tatare-to po gorody pokhazivayut,
Little did they know what Tsar Ivan had in store;	Na tsarya Ivana-to poglyadyvayut,
How they'd shout and roar!	Zli tatarove.

(He drinks.)

Now Ivan puts on his well-known frown.	Grozny tsar-ot zakruchinilsa,
Head on shoulder, our Tsar is busy working out a plan.	On povyesil golovushku na pravoe plecho.
All at once he calls his gunner boys,	Uzh kak stal tsar pushkaryey szyvat',
And he bids them stand with fuse in hand,	Pushkaryey vsye zazhigal'shchikov.
Stand with fuse in hand.	Zazhigal'shchikov!
Now the fuses of candle-wax are set alight.	Zadymilasa svyechka vosku yarova,
One young gunner goes up and gives the casks a push.	Podkhodil molodoy pushkar-ot k bochechke.
See the barrels full of powder start to roll and roll.	A i s porokhom-to bochka zakruzhilasya,
Hoy! Down the tunnel see them tumbling to their goal,	Oy, po podkopam pokatilasya,
With a bang explode!	Da i khlopnula.

(He drinks.)

How they howl, those wicked Tartars as they're blown on high!	Zavopili, zagaldili zli tatarove,
How they shriek and yell with all their might!	Blagim matom zalivalisya.
Tartar bodies strew the fortress far and wide.	Poleglo tatarovey t'ma t'mushchaya,
Corpses numbered twenty hundred score, And three thousand more!	Poleglo ikh sorok tysyachey, i tri tysyachi.
Such was the fate of Kazan	Tak-to vo gorode bylo,
The mighty fortress! Hoy!	Vo Kazani. E!

(He takes a long draught. Then to Grigory)

Why are you not singing with me,	Shtozh ty nye podtyagivaesh,
and why aren't you drinking with me?	Da i nye potyagivaesh?

GRIGORY

I don't want to.	Nye khochu.

Each to his fancy!   Vol'nomu volya.

And mine is for wine, my good Missail.   A pyanomu ray, otyets Misail!
Drink a toast with me   Vypyem charochku
to our hostess here!   Za shinkarochku!
(*He fills two glasses; the two drink. Varlaam stares at Grigory, then addresses him with drunken gaiety.*)
But listen, friend: Odnako, brat,
when I've a thirst,   Kogda ya pyu,
let sober men be cursed!   Tak trezvykh nye lyublyu;
                    (*He drinks.*)
I've no use for thinkers,   Ino dyelo pyanstvo,
I like honest drinkers.   Ino dyelo chvanstvo;
If you'd live like us   Khochesh zhit' kak my,
you're welcome young fellow!   Milosti prosim!
If not, then go your own way,   Nyet! tak ubiraysa,
to hell with you!   Provalivay!

Drink, but keep your thoughts to yourself,   Pyey, da pro sebya razumyey,
my good Varlaam!   Otyets Varlaam!

To myself!   Pro sebya!
Why should I keep my thoughts to myself?   Da shto mnye pro sebya razumyet'?
                    (*annoyed*)
Ah! He walks along, walks all day long,   [13] Ekh! Kak yedet yon, yedet yon, yon . . .
Singing a merry song.   Da pogonyaet yon.
                (*He sprawls on the table. Missail dozes.*)
He can't go wrong, the journey is long,   Shapka na yom torchit kak rozhon,
Yet the ale was very strong!   Vyes, akh, vyes to gryazyon!

(*going to the Hostess*)

Good hostess, that road out there, where   Khozyayka! Kuda vedyot eta doroga?
does it lead to?

Lithuania, sir.   A v Litvu, kormilets.

Is the frontier very far?   A dalyeche do Litvy?

No, young fellow, it's quite near here: Nyet, rodimy, nye dalyeche.
you'd easily get there by dark   K vyecheru mozhnob pospyet',
once you've passed the sentries.   Kaby nye zastavy.

What? Are there sentries?   Kak? Zastavy?

Someone from Moscow's escaped,   Kto-to bezhal iz Moskvy,
so now they must stop all travellers, and   A vyeleno vsyekh zadyerzhivat', da
  examine them.   osmatrivat'.

Ah! Well, hostess, this is not my lucky day!   E! Vot tebye, babushka, i Yuryev dyen!

(*waking*) [13]

Now he falls down,   Svalilsa yon
Bumping his crown.   Lezhit yon, yon.

	(falling asleep)
Yet all he does is frown.	Da vstat' nye mozhet yon.
	(He sleeps.)

GRIGORY

| Who's the man they're after? | A kovo im nuzhno? |

HOSTESS

| Couldn't tell you. Who knows, some robber perhaps, | Uzh nye znayu. Vor li, razboynik kakoy. |
| that's why the road is barred by the police, confound them! | Tol'ko prokhodu nyet ot pristavov proklyatykh! |

GRIGORY
(thoughtfully)

| So ... | Tak ... |

HOSTESS

What's the point of it all?	A chevo poymayut?
He'll get by, they'll never capture him.	Nichevo, ni byesa lysavo!
There are other ways to go besides the highway.	Budto tol'ko i puti, shto stolbovaya!

(confidentially)

Look: I can show you.	Vot, khot' otsuda:
Turn up on the left there;	Svoroti nalyevo,
follow the footpath	Da po tropinke,
till you come to the chapel at Chekhan,	I idi do Chekanskoy chasovni
it's near a stream,	Shto na ruchyu;
and from there go to Khlopino,	A ottuda na Khlopino,
and then to Zaytsevo,	A tam na Zaytsevo;
and from then on even a schoolboy	A tut uzh vsyakiy mal'chishka
knows the way to Lithuania.	Do Litvy tebya provodit ...
These sentries spend their time	Ot etikh pristavov
looking for trouble; they annoy the travellers	Tol'ko i tolku. Shto tyesnyat prokhozhikh,
and so they make us all suffer!	Da obirayut nas byednykh ...

VARLAAM
(yawning and stretching himself; in his sleep) [13]

Comes to his door:	Priyekhal yon,
Knocks hard, knock, knock!	Da v dvyer tuk! tuk!
	(quiet knocking at the door)
Calls out and knocks the more,	Da shto yest' mochenki
	(half waking)
Knock, knock, knock!	Tuk! tuk! tuk!

(louder knocking)

HOSTESS
(listening)

Now who is there?	Shto tam yeshcho?
	(She goes to the window and looks out carefully.)
Here they are, the cursed ones,	Vot oni proklyatyye!
they're back again on patrol!	Opyat' dozorom idut!

She opens the door. Enter Police Officers who stand by the door and observe the travellers. The Hostess zealously makes a deep bow to them. [2a]

VARLAAM
(waking and then becoming drowsy again) [13]

He's on the floor,	Kak yedet yon,
Can't even snore,	Yedet yon, yon,
His nose is too sore.	Da pogonyaet ...

POLICE OFFICER

| Right, who are you lot? | Vy shto za lyudi? |

MISSAIL AND VARLAAM
(Both jump up in haste, startled. Piously.) [11]

God-fearing mendicants, venerable friars, wandering through the country collecting alms for charity, sir.	Startsy smiryennyye, inoki chestnyye Khodim po selyeniyam, sobiraem milostynku.

POLICE OFFICER
(to Grigory)

Who're you, in that case?	A ty kto takoy?

MISSAIL AND VARLAAM
(quickly)

Our companion.	Nash tovarishch.

GRIGORY
(He goes boldly to the Officer, and says casually:) [9]

I come from the town over there . . . I've been showing these friars the way;	Miryanin iz prigoroda . . . Provodil startsev do rubyezha . . .

(with a bow)

and soon I'll be going.	Idu vo svoyasi.

(The Police Officers confer in whispers.)

POLICE OFFICER
(to his companion)

Nothing to get out of him: he's broke, most likely . . . but as for these two . . . Hum!	Paren-to, kazhetsa, gol: Plokha pozhiva . . . Vot razve startsy . . . Hm!

(He clears his throat, goes to the table and sits down.)

Well, your reverence, and how's business with you today?	Nu, otsy moi, kakovo promyshlyaete?

VARLAAM

Oh, dreadful, brother, dreadful! Christian folk are misers nowadays, love their money, try to hoard it, little's rendered to God. Yea, sin and corruption have attained their dominion. Walking's useless, talking's useless; begging, praying, all we get's a coin or two. What's left but sorrow and so we drink all we take. Ah, the dread judgement of God cannot be delayed!	Okh! plokho, syne, plokho! Khristiane skupy stali, Dyengu lyubyat, dyengu pryachut, Malo Bogu dayut. Priide grekh veliy Na yazystsy zemli. Khodish, khodish, molish, molish, Yele, yele tri polushki vymolish. Shto dyelat'? S gorya i ostal'noe propyosh. Okh, prishli nashi poslyedniye vryemena!

HOSTESS
(to herself, plaintively)

Lord above have mercy and protect us!	Gospodi pomiluy i spasi nas!

(While Varlaam speaks, the Officer examines him attentively. Varlaam, sensing that he is being watched, becomes uneasy.)

VARLAAM

Why is it you stare and watch me so closely?	Shto ty na menya tak pristal'no smotrish?

POLICE OFFICER

I'll tell you!	[2a] A vot shto:

(to his companion)

Alyokha, got the warrant there?	Alyokha! pri tebye ukas?

(He takes the paper and addresses Varlaam.)

Well, give it to me! Listen: there has fled from Moscow a certain wicked monk, Grishka Otrepiev. Had you ever heard that?	Davay suda! Vidish: iz Moskvy bezhal Nyekiy eretik, Grishka Otryepev. Znaesh li ty eto?

VARLAAM
(humbly)

No, never.   Nye znayu.

POLICE OFFICER

Well, the Tsar has ordered us to have him caught
and then hanged on the gallows.
D'you know about that then?

Nu, i tsar velyel yevo, eretika,
Izlovit' i povyesit'.
Slykhal li ty eto?

VARLAAM

No, I don't.   Nye slykhal.

POLICE OFFICER

Can you read?   Chitat' umyeesh?

VARLAAM

No, brother, I never got that far!   Nyet, syne, nye umudril gospod'.

POLICE OFFICER
(He hands the warrant to Varlaam.)

Well, take a look at this.   Tak, vot tebye ukaz!

VARLAAM
(startled, and without taking the warrant)

What's it to me?   Na shto on mnye?

POLICE OFFICER

This much, that the base heretic monk must be you!

Etot eretik, razboynik, vor, Grishka — ty!

VARLAAM

Absurd! How can you say such things?   Vona! shto ty, gospod's toboy!

HOSTESS
(aside)

Lord above, they even try to persecute the fathers!

Gospodi! i startsa-to v pokoye nye ostavyat!

OFFICER

Right, who can read me this?   Ey! Kto zdyes gramotny?

(All stare at one another, silently.)

GRIGORY
(going to the Officer)

I'll read it out.   Ya gramotny.

POLICE OFFICER
(disconcerted)

Really!   Eva!
(He gives the warrant to Grigory.)
Well, begin; slowly now!   Nu, chitay . . . Vslukh chitay!

GRIGORY
(reading)

'At the cloister of Chudov
an irreverent monk by name one Grigory Otrepiev,
has succumbed to wickedness,
and striven to tempt the holy brotherhood with devious
forms of blandishments and profanities.
As he's now attempting to reach Lithuania,
the Tsar has decreed that you catch the man' . . .

Chudova monastyrya
nedostoyny chernyets Grigory, iz rodu Otryepyevykh,
nauchon diavolum;
vzdumal smushchat' svyatuyu bratiyu
vsyakimi soblazny i bezzakoniyami.
A bezhal on, Grishka,
k granitse Litovskoy,
i tsar prikazal izlovit' yevo' . . .

68

And then hang him! | I povyesit'.

(to Police Officer)

Here there's nothing about hanging. | Zdyes nye skazano povyesit'.

Liar! It's there between the lines, I'm sure of it. | Vryosh! nye vsyako slovo v stroku pishetsa.

Go on: you must catch and then hang him. | Chitay: Izlovit', i povyesit'.

And then hang him. | I povyesit'.
(reading)

'The age of this ... | A lyet yemu ...
(stealthily considering Varlaam)

Grishka is about fifty-five ... | Grishke ... ot rodu pyatdesyat ...
His build is rather stout, his beard is grey, | boroda sedaya,
and his nose purple' ... | bryukho tolstoe, nos krasny' ...

Get hold of him! It's him we're after! | Derzhi yevo! Derzhi, rebyata!

All rush towards Varlaam, who quickly pushes them away.

(with fists clenched and striking a pugnacious attitude)

Hold it! Have all of you gone mad in here? | Shto vy! Postryeli okayannyye!
Just think a little! How could I be Grishka? | Chevo pristali? Nu, kakoy ya Grishka?
(He tears the paper out of Grigory's hands.)
No, friend, someone's having a joke! | Nyet, brat, molod shutki shutit'!
Although I'm poor at reading, | Khot' po skladam umyeyu,
and slow to find the meaning, | Khot' plokho razbirayu,
I'll spell it out, spell it out, | A razberu! razberu!
since now it seems a matter for hanging! | Kak dyelo-to do pyetli dokhodit.
(reading but stumbling over the words)
'And his age ... his age is about ... | 'A lye ... lyet ... a lyet yemu ...
(looking intently at the paper)
twenty!' | Dvadtsat'!
(to Grigory)
Where's your fifty-five? Nowhere! | Gdyezh tut pyatdesyat? Vidish!
(He reads. Grigory creeps closer to the door.)
'He's slender and fairly tall, | 'A rostu on sryednevo
red-haired and ... | Volosy ... ryzhiye.
on his nose there is a ... is a wart | Na nosu ... na nosu borodavka.
and another on his ... forehead. | Na lbu ... drugaya.
(Grigory is at the window, one hand to his chest.)
Also his left arm ... left arm ... is not as | Odna ruka ... ruka koroche ... koroche
long as his right arm' ... | drugoy' ...
(staring at Grigory and then walking up to him)
Why, surely that is ... | Da, eto uzh nye ...

Grigory pulls out a knife and jumps through the window. All, startled, stare at the window but do not move from their places.

That's him, that's him, get hold of him! | Derzhi, derzhi yevo, derzhi yevo!

After a moment's hesitation, they recover from their shock and rush through the door, shouting 'Stop thief!'.

Curtain.

Act Two

A sumptuously furnished room in the Imperial Palace in the Moscow Kremlin. Xenia is weeping over her fiancé's portrait. The Tsarevich is studying a map. The Nurse sits sewing. On the left, in the corner, stands a chiming clock.

XENIA

Where are you, dearest,	[14] Gdye ty, zhenikh moy;
where are you, beloved?	Gdye ty, moy zhelanny!
In the cold earth lying,	Vo syroy mogilke,
in a distant country.	Na chuzhoy storonke;
You lie all alone there	Lezhish odinoko,
in darkness for ever.	Pod kamnem tyazholym ...
Not seeing my sorrow,	Nye vidish ty skorbi,
not hearing my weeping.	Nye slyshish ty placha,
Weeping and mourning,	Placha golubki,
alone I must languish ...	Kak ty, odinokoy.

(She weeps.)

FYODOR

Xenia! Don't cry, dear sister!	Kseniya! nye plach, golubka!
Grief like yours is bitter,	Gore lyuto, pravda,
but neither crying nor mourning	Da nye slezami, nye voplem
will help you drive away your sorrow ...	Izbudesh tyazhkuyu kruchinu ...

XENIA

Ah, Fyodor!	Akh, Fyodor!
He's left me for ever;	Nye mnye on dostalsa,
death has taken him from me!	a siroy mogilke!
I will mourn for ever;	Nyet mnye bol'she schastya,
all my life will be sorrow ...	Noet byednoe serdtse ...

FYODOR

Don't be sad or despondent,	Nye tomis, nye kruchinsa,
Xenia, dear sister.	Kseniya, golubka!

(pointing to the clock)

Oh look! The clock's begun.	Glyadi-ko! chasy poshli!
The bells have started chiming.	Kuranty zaigrali!

(leading Xenia towards it)

It's a very old, special, clock,	A pro tye chasy pisano:

(The Nurse looks at the clock.)

every hour, and every quarter and half,	Kak chasy i perechasya zabyut,
quite suddenly, all the little instruments start playing,	I v tye pory v truby i vargany zaigrayut,
the drums beat and people appear ...	I v nakry, i lyudy vykhodyat, i lyudi tye ...
Look, there they are ...	

(to the Nurse)

Watch them, Nanny, just like live ones, look!	Glyan-ko, mama, kak zhivyye, vish!

XENIA

I'll never forget you,	Zhenikh ty moy, mily.
dearest prince among princes!	Mily moy, Korolyevich!
My heart is breaking all for you, beloved.	Toskuyet serdtse pro tebye, zhelanny!

(She weeps. The Nurse spits and turns briskly to Xenia.)

NURSE

Enough! Stop this Tsarevna, my dearest one.	Au! Polno, tsaryevna, golubushka!
Weep no longer, your grief will kill you!	Polno plakat', da ubivat'sa.

XENIA

I'm wretched, Nanny dear, so wretched . . .	Akh, grustno, mamushka, tak grustno!

NURSE

Come now, think no more of him . . .	I, shto ty, dityatko!
Maiden's tears are like the dew upon the grass;	Dyevichi slyozy, shto rosa:
once the sun shines the grass soon is dry again!	Vzyodyot solnyshko, rosu vysushit.
There's all the world to choose from!	Nye klinom svyet sosholsa.
We'll find another bridegroom,	Naydyom my zhenikha,
such a handsome one, such a wonderful one!	I prigozhevo, i privyetlivo . . .
You'll soon forget Ivan and live in happiness.	Zabudesh pro Ivana Korolyevicha . . .

XENIA

Oh, no, no, Nanny dear!	Akh, nyet, nyet, mamushka!
I'll be true to him even although he'd dead.	Ya i myortvomu budu yemu, verna.

NURSE

Nonsense! You weren't wed to him,	Vot kak! mel'kom videla,
Why still mourn for him?	Uzh issokhnula . . .
Once there lived a maid who pined away,	Skushno bylo dyevitse odnoy,
till she chanced to fall in love one day;	Polyubilsa molodyets likhoy.
when her lover died, I've heard it tell,	Kak nye stalo molodtsa tovo,
vows were soon forgot, and all was well.	Razlyubila dyevitsa yevo.
There, my darling, that's the way of wisdom;	Ekh, golubka, to-to tvoyo gore!
set grief aside, and hear	Luchshe prislushaykas,
the song I'm going to sing!	Shto ya tebye skazhu:
While the gnat was chopping wood [15]	Kak komar drova rubil,
And working as good gnats should,	Komar vodu vozil,
In her kitchen the flea	Klopik tyesto mesil,
Cooked him something for his tea.	Komaru obyed nosil.
At that time a dragonfly	Maletyela strekoza,
Happened to be passing by;	Na dyakovy na luga,
Scattered all the farmer's hay,	I davay krutit', mutit',
Down the stream it whirled away.	Syeno v ryeku vorotit'.
Gnat was in a rage,	Oserchal komar
Started to rampage,	Za dyakov tovar:
Saw the dragonfly retreating,	Pobezhal byegom za syenom,
Took a log and started beating.	Stal gonyat' strekoz polyenom.
But, alas, he missed his stroke,	Na komaryu na bedu,
And the heavy cudgel broke.	To polyeno sorvalos,
As it hit him, gnat went flying;	Po strekozam yeye popalo,
Broke his back and lay there dying.	Ryobra komaru slomalo.
Hearing of the poor gnat's plight,	Na podmogushku yemu,
Flea arose when day was light;	Ranym rano, po utru,
Hurried to her neighbour's aid,	Klop lopatu privolok.
Tried to lift him with a spade.	Komaru pod samy bok.
But her efforts were in vain,	Da nye vzduzhil, iznemog,
Flea could never stand the strain;	Komara podnyat' nye smog.
Feebly she began to nod,	Zhivotochek nadorval . . .
Rendered up her soul to God.	Bogu dushenku otdal . . .

FYODOR

Oh, really, Nanny dear, what a song to sing!	Ekh, mama, mamushka, vot kak skazochka!
The start was gay, but the end was very sad!	Vela za zdravye, svela za upokoy!

NURSE

Well then, Tsarevich, tell a better one;	Nishto, tsaryevich! Al' poluchshe znaesh?
let's hear it, now; and I shall listen patiently.	Pokhvastaykas! My slushat' terpelivy,
I can behave myself for Tsar Ivan	My vyed, u batyushki Tsarya Ivana
made me patient and obedient. Well now!	Terpenyu obuchalis. Nu-kas!

FYODOR

Oh, Nanny, I'm sure you'll like my song,	Oy, mama! smotri, nye vyterpish!
and you must sing too!	Sama podtyanesh.

(The game of hand-clapping. Fyodor makes the Nurse play with him. They both dance round in circles, clapping their hands rhythmically, and trying to reach and smack one another.)

Here's a song to make people laugh, [16]	Skazochka pro to i pro syo:
How once a speckled hen hatched a calf,	Kak kurochka bychka rodila.
How a piglet laid a big brown egg.	Porosyonochek yaichko snyos.
Take it or leave it; many folk believe it.	Skazka poyotsa, durnyam nye dayotsa.

(He rises, stands before the Nurse, and while singing claps his hands, once to each bar.)

Cock-a-doodle little bird,	Turu, turu, petushok,
I can watch you as you fly,	Ty dalyoko l' otoshol?
Far away across the sea,	Za more, za more,
Overland to Kiev town.	K Kievu gorodu.
There's an oak stands proud and lofty;	Tam dub stoit razvyesisty,
On the oak sits an owl wise and crafty.	Na dubu sych sidit uvyesisty.

FYODOR AND NURSE

See him wink his eyes,	Sych glazom morgnyot,
Hear him as he cries:	Sych pyesnu poyot:
Too-hoo, whit-a-woo,	Dzin, dzin, peredzin.
Watch me winking, watch me blinking;	Postriguli, pomiguli,
Ding-dong, sing a song,	Tyen, tyen potetyen,
Topsy-turvy all day long!	Za kolodu da na pyen!
Toes a-tapping, hands a-clapping!	Shagom, magom, chetvertagom.

FYODOR

To our village, one fine day,	Kak odnova na selye
Came a sparrow small and gay,	Zarodili vorobya:
And as some alleged,	Sovsyem vorobyey,
Only newly fledged.	Sovsyem molodoy:
See his long pointed beak,	Klinonosenky,
Feathered coat, brown and sleek.	Vostronosenky.
Sparrow soon flew away	Poletyel vorobyey,
With the wise owl to stay,	Pryamo v gosti k sychu.
Whispering low in his ear	Stal sheptat' na ushko
Thus he told him:	Usatomu.

NURSE

Boys from the village were threshing the barley,	Parni dyakovy molotili,
When all of a sudden they noticed a fire.	Tsepy polomali, vovin pobrosali,

(Fyodor and the Nurse gradually come towards each other.)

The flames started leaping higher and higher.	Ovin zagoryelsa, polymen pyshet,
Sexton likewise saw the black smoke arise.	Dyaku v okno stalo vidno yevo.

FYODOR AND NURSE

Sexton is frightened and hides by a boulder,	Dyak ispugalsa, zalyez pod kadushku,
But bruises his shoulder;	Shchemil sebye ushko . . .

FYODOR

Someone sees him, all his friends tease him.	Pisar, s pechi, oborval plechi
Sexton's mother bakes every day forty cakes.	Dyakova zhena kalachey napekla.
But the watchmen on the run	Nabezhali pristava,
Came and swallowed every one,	Vsye poyeli kalachi . . .

FYODOR AND NURSE

And the fattest ate two oxen and a cow,	Sam nabol'shy syel korovu, da byka,
Ten pigs and a bull;	Semsot porosyat,
Yet he still wasn't full . . .	Odni nozhki visyat.

(Fyodor smacks the Nurse on her shoulder.)

Touch! Khlyost!

(Enter Boris. Seeing him, the Nurse curtsies deeply.)

NURSE

Mercy! Akh ty!

(Fyodor goes to the table, sits down, and resumes his work.)

BORIS

What's this? Am I a wolf, that frights the   Chevo? Al lyuty zvyer nasyedku
broody hen?   vspolokhnul?

NURSE

Mightiest Tsar, forgive me: Tsar, gosudar, pomiluy!
old age has made me frail and rather   Pod starost'-to pugliva bol'no stala.
nervous.

(Boris goes to Xenia and puts his arm round her.)

BORIS

My Xenia, dry your tears, my darling.   Shto, Kseniya? shto byednaya golubka!
Though left before your wedding as a widow,   V nevyestakh uzh pechal'naya vdovitsa!
your weeping and distress are all in vain.   Vsyo plachesh ty o myortvom zhenikhe.

XENIA

O my good lord, don't let these foolish tears   O gosudar! nye ogorchaysa ty slezoy
of mine distress you.   devichey!
A maiden's grief is surely but a trifle   Devichye gore tak lekhko, nichtozhno
compared with your great burden.   Pyered tvoyeyu skorbyu.

BORIS
(caressing Xenia) [17]

My Xenia, beloved daughter!   Ditya moyo! moya golubka!
Go to your chamber now, and talk with   Besyedoy tyoployu, s podrugami v svetlitse,
your companions,
and so forget this deep affliction.   Rassyey svoy um ot dum tyazholykh.
(He kisses her.)
Now go, my child!   Idi, ditya!
(Exit Xenia with her Nurse; Boris watches her as she goes. Then he approaches his son.)
And you, my son, still working?   A ty, moy syn, chem zanyat?
(seeing the map)
What's this I see?   Eto shto?

FYODOR

The map of great Moscovia,   Chertyozh zemli Moskovskoy,
our dominion from end to end.   Nashe tsarstvo, iz kraya v kray.
(pointing)
I'll show you: here is Moscow,   [18] Vot vidish: vot Moskva,
here's Novgorod, and here's Kazan,   Vot Novgorod, a vot Kazan, Astrakhan.
Astrakhan;
the Caspian, yes, the Caspian,   Vot more, Kaspiy more;
and here's the endless forest-land of Perm,   Vot Permskiye dremuchiye lesa.
and here's Siberia.   A vot Sibir.

BORIS

How well explained, my son!   Kak khorosho, moy syn!
As from on high with all before you   Kak s oblakov, yedinym vzorom,
you're able to survey our kingdom: Ty mozhesh obozret' vsyo tsarstvo:
its frontiers, rivers, cities.   Granitsy, reki, grady.
Work hard, Fyodor!   Uchis, Fyodor!
A time will come (who knows, it may be [35]   Kogda-nibud', i skoro mozhet byt',
soon)
when you, you shall inherit this realm of   Tebye vsyo eto tsarstvo dostanetsa.
ours . . .
Work hard, my son!   Uchis, ditya.

(Fyodor goes up-stage and returns to his studies. Boris goes to the table and sits deep in thought, turning over the scrolls and parchments.) [7]

I stand supreme in power.	Dostig ya vyshey vlasti.
Five years and more my reign has been untroubled.	Shestoy uzh god ya tsarstvuyu spokoyno.
And yet I grieve within my sad, tormented soul!	No schastya nyet moyey izmuchennoy dushe!
In vain the wise astrologers foretell	[19] Naprasno mnye kudyesniki sudyat
long life and years of glory, free from turmoil.	Dni dolgie, dni vlasti bezmyatyezhnoy.
Nor life, nor power,	Ni zhizn, ni vlast',
nor transient lure of glory,	Ni slavy obol'shchenya,
nor praise from the crowds	Ni kliki tolpy
can cheer my aching heart.	Menya nye veselyat!
My children might have brought me consolation.	V semye svoyey ya mnil nayti otradu,
I planned a feast to greet my daughter as a bride,	Gotovil docheri vesyoly brachny pir,
my sweet Tsarevna, my cherished angel.	Moyey tsaryevne, golubke chistoy.
Like lightning death has struck the one she loved.	Kak burya, smyert' unosit zhenikha . . .
How fearful is the wrath of God on high,	[20] Tyazhka desnitsa groznovo Sudii,
how merciless a doom awaits the guilty!	Uzhasen prigovor dushe prestupnoy . . .
Eternal gloom and darkness surround me,	Okrest lish t'ma i mrak neproglyadny!
Oh could one ray of hope but cheer me!	Khotya mel'knul by luch otrady!
My heart is sick with anguish,	[19] I skorbyu serdtse polno,
my spirit is torn and racked with suffering.	Toskuyet, tomitsa dukh ustaly.
A secret terror haunts me;	Kakoy-to tryepet tayny,
some dread consumes me . . .	Vsyo zhdyosh chevo-to
In contrite prayer I implore saints and angels	Molitvoy tyoploy k ugodnikam bozhym,
to bring me release from all my torment.	Ya mnil zaglushit' dushi stradanya . . .
Though seated in royal splendour, Tsar of Russia,	V velichy i blyeske vlasti bezgranichnoy,
I kneel before them, and in tears appeal for consolation.	Rusi vladyka, ya slyoz prosil mnye v uteshenye.
But God condemns and sends rebellion,	A tam donos: boyar kramola,
plots and intrigues, conspiracies in Poland.	Kozni Litvy, i taynye podkopy,
Death, disease, and villainy surround me;	Glad, i mor, i trus, i razzorenye . . .
pestilence and famine have ravaged my kingdom.	Slovno diky zvyer ryshchet lyud zachumlyonny:
Impoverished, destitute, Russia groans.	Golodnaya, byednaya stonet Rus . . .
And all who suffer this vengeance of heaven	[20] I v lyutom gore, nisposlannom bogom,
believe in their hearts I am guilty.	Za tyazhky moy gryekh v ispytanye,
They lay the blame on me for their sorrows,	Vinoy vsyekh zol menya narekayut,
the name of Tsar Boris rouses their hatred.	Klyanut na ploshchadyakh imya Borisa!
And even sleep has fled,	[21] I dazhe son bezhit,
for now every night-time	I v sumrake nochi
a child appears, his face congealed with blood.	Ditya okrovavlyonnoe vstayut . . .
Sobbing in anguish, clenching his fists,	Ochi pylayut stisnuv ruchonki,
he begs me for mercy,	Prosit poshchady . . .
but mercy was denied him!	I nye bylo poshchady!
Freshly his wound is gaping,	Strashnaya rana ziyaet!
loudly he cries as death enshrouds him . . .	Slyshitsa krik yevo predsmyertny . . .

(He rises abruptly and sinks down again heavily.)

O God above, pity me!	O gospodi, bozhe moy!

NURSES
(off-stage yelling)

Ah, shoo!	Ay, kysh!

BORIS
(anxiously)

Now what's happened?	Shto takoe?

Ah, shoo, shoo! Rascal! Ay, kysh, kysh! Akhti!

BORIS
(to his son, loudly and angrily)

Go at once, find out what's happened! Uznay, shto tam sluchilos!

(Exit Fyodor.)

NURSES

Shoo, shoo! Ah! Kysh, kysh! Ay!

BORIS
(greatly annoyed)

Lord, what a noise! Ek, voyut-to!

NURSES

Shoo! Shoo! Shoo! You wicked bird! Kysh! Kysh! Kysh! Oy, likhonka!

(Enter the Boyar in attendance; he makes a deep obeisance with arms extended.)

BORIS
(to the Boyar)

What is it? Ty, zachem?

NURSES

Shoo! Shoo! Kysh! Kysh!

BORIS
(watching the Boyar closely, with assumed calm)

Where's your tongue? Speak! Shtozh molchish? Nu!

BOYAR

Most mighty lord and Tsar! Veliky gosudar!
Outside Prince Vassily Shuisky craves Tebye knyaz Vasily Shuysky chelom byot.
  audience.

BORIS

Shuisky? All right! Shuysky? Zovi!
Go say we're glad to see His Highness Skazhi, shto rady videt' knyazya
and wait to hear his tidings. I zhdyom yevo besyedy.

BOYAR
(He rises and whispers in the Tsar's ear.)

Last night one of Pushkin's serfs Vechor, Pushkina kholop
informed against him, and testified Prishol's donosom na Shuyskovo
that Shuisky and his master, with other Mstislavskovo i prochikh i na khozyayna:
  noblemen,
sat in secret conversation half the night; Nochyu taynaya besyeda shla u nikh,
at dawn a messenger from Krakov brought Gonyets iz Krakovo priyekhal i privyoz ...
  them news ...

BORIS
(angrily)

Arrest the man! Gontsa skhvatit'!

(Exit Boyar. Re-enter Fyodor.)

BORIS

Aha, Prince Shuisky! Akha, Shuysky knyaz!
(to Fyodor, anxiously)
What was it? What made those stupid Nu shto? S chevo tam dury baby vzvyli?
  women cry out so?

FYODOR

Our parrot. Vsyo popka nash.

Parrot?

Popka?

FYODOR

O my father, do not ask me any more,
why should I trouble you with such a
    stupid story?

Nye prigozhe bylob, otche gosudar,
Um tvoy derzhavny utruzhdat' rasskazom
    vzdornym.

BORIS

No, speak, my child!
What was it? Tell your story.

Nyet, nyet, ditya!
Vsyo, slyshish, vsyo, kak bylo.

(He caresses his son. Fyodor sits on the floor and tells his tale, leaning on his father's knees.)

FYODOR

Polly was in our room,	[22] Popinka nash sidyel
sitting with the nurses,	S mamkami v svetlitse,
cheerful and well-behaved,	Byez umolku boltal,
chattering without ceasing.	Vyesel byl i laskov,
Coyly he bent his head,	K mamushkam podkhodil,
and bowing this and that way,	Prosil chesat' golovku,
offered it to the nurses	K kazhdoy on podkhodil,
each in turn to scratch it.	Cheryod im soblyudaya.
Nanny Nastasia	Mamka Nastasya
refused to pet and scratch him.	Chesat' nye zakhotela,
Polly became annoyed,	Popinka, oserdyas,
told her she was ugly.	Nazval mamku duroy.
Nanny was very cross,	Mamka, s obidy shtol'
seized him by the collar,	Khvat' yevo po sheyke,
Polly began to shriek,	Popka kak zakrichit,
ruffled up his feathers.	Dybom vstali pyerya.
Then just to keep him quiet	Nu yevo blazhat',
someone offered him a biscuit;	Ugoshchat' yevo slastyami,
soon every other nurse	Vsyem prichetom molit',
was trying hard to calm him.	Laskat' yevo, pokoit'.

BORIS

Stupid women!

Nu, uzh, dury!

FYODOR

But wait! There's more to follow.
Sulking and looking cross,
Polly won't be tempted —

Da nyet, nye tut to bylo!
Khmury takoy sidit,
Nos utknuvshi v pyerya —

BORIS

No wonder!

Yeshcho by!

FYODOR

Won't take his favourite sweets,	Na slasti nye glyadit,
only sits and grumbles.	Shto-to vsyo bormochet ...
Then all at once he jumps	Vdrug k mamke podskochil,
and lands on nurse Nastasia,	Chesat' shto nye khotyela,
bites her and starts to scratch;	Davay yeyo dolbit',
nurse jumps back and tumbles over.	Ta i grokhnulasa ob pol.
Now everyone goes wild —	Tut mamki, so strastyey,
nanny's in a frenzy;	Slovno vzbelenilis,
shrieking and waving arms,	Stali makhat', krichat',
all attempt to capture Polly.	Popinku zagnat' khotyeli.
But Polly won;	Da nye vprosak,
each of them was taught a lesson.	Popka kazhduyu otmyetil.
So, father, now you know	Vot, otche gosudar,
the reason for the shouting,	Oni, glyadish, i vzvyli,
that is why you were disturbed	Dumu tsarskuyu tvoyu
deep in meditation.	Dumat' pomeshali.
There, I think that's all:	Vot, kazhis, i vsyo,
that's what happened.	Vsyo kak bylo.

BORIS
(He caresses his son lovingly.)

My son, my well-beloved Fyodor!	Moy syn, ditya moyo rodnoye!
Who could be prouder than I am	S kakim isskustvom, kak boyko
at hearing you tell your story?	Ty vyol svoy rasskaz pravdivy;
How simply and yet with what humour	Kak prosto, bezkhitrostno, lovko
you pictured the scene, just as it happened.	Sumyel opisat' sluchay potyeshny,
Sweet is the fruit of learning:	Vot sladky plod uchenya,
cultivate knowledge, it will never fail you.	Istiny svyetom, uma okrylyenye.
Oh, if I could but live to see you Tsar of Russia,	O, yesli by ya mog tebya Tsaryom uvidet',
the rightful monarch of this empire!	Rusi pravitelem derzhavnym,
Ah, yes were it granted that I should know such blessing,	O, s kakim vostorgom presryev soblazny vlasti
then I would gladly renounce all glory, crown and sceptre!	Na to blazhenstvo ya promenyal by posokh tsarsky.
But be warned, my son, and when you're crowned as monarch	No kogda, ditya, pravitelem ty stanesh,
reflect, and try to choose advisers who are trusty.	Staraysa izbirat' sovyetnikov nadyozhnykh;
Beware of Shuisky and examine his counsel;	Boysa Shuyskovo izvyetov kovarnykh,

(Enter Shuisky.)

he seems so loyal, but he's sly and false ...	Sovyetnik mudry, no lukav i zol ...

SHUISKY
(making a deep obeisance)

Most mighty Lord and Tsar, my homage!	Veliky gosudar, chelom byu.

BORIS
(with a start)

Ah, the demagogue himself,	A, preslavny vitiya,
the worthy one to lead the brainless rabble,	Dostoiny konovod tolpy bezmozgloy;
the spokesman of my sly, seditious boyars,	Prestupnaya glava boyar kramol'nykh,
wiliest of traitors to your Tsar!	Tsarskovo prestola supostat.
Brazen liar, thrice forsworn and ever-lying,	Nagly lzhets, trizhdy klyatvu prestupivshy,
hypocrite and knave, adulator,	Khitry litsemyer, l'styets lukavy,
you, Judas, you rogue disguised as boyar,	Prosvirnya pod shapkoyu boyarskoy,
impostor, snake!	Obmanshchik, plut!

SHUISKY

Under Tsar Ivan (may God Almighty grant him mercy!),	Pri tsarye Ivane (pokoy gospodi yevo dushu),
Prince Vassily Shuisky was esteemed according to his lineage.	Shuyskiye knyazya nye tyem pochotom otlichalis.

BORIS

What? Why, Tsar Ivan Vassilich the Terrible	Shto? Da Tsar, Ivan Vasilych Grozny,
would cheerfully have burnt you at the stake for less!	Okhotno by tebya na ugol'kakh podzharil,
Yes, and stretching out his royal sceptre	Sam, svoyeyu tsarskoyu desnitsey,
have fanned the leaping flames, stirred the glowing embers,	Vorochal vy na nikh posokhom zhelyeznym,
and sung in thanks a holy anthem ...	Psalom svyashchenny napevaya.
But we are kinder, and suffer patiently	A my nye gordy, nam lyubo milovat',
your arrogance and treason.	Nadmyennovo kholopa.

SHUISKY
(angrily)

Tsar!	Tsar!

BORIS
(derisively)

Yes? What is it, worthy Prince?	Shto? Shto skazhesh, Shuysky knyaz?

SHUISKY
(submissively)

Tsar!	Tsar . . .
	(coming close to Boris)
I bring tidings,	Yest . . .vyesti,
and most important ones relating to your throne . . .	I vyesti vazhnye dlya tsarstva tvoyevo.

BORIS

Which only yesterday,	Nye tyel', shto Pushkinu,
a secret messenger	Ili tebye tam, shtol',
conveyed to you at Pushkin's	Privyoz posol potayny
from your accomplices,	Ot sopriyatelyey,
the traitorous boyars?	Boyar opal'nykh?

SHUISKY
(boldly)

Yes, mighty Tsar!	Da, gosudar!
From Poland comes news of a pretender.	V Litvye yavilsa Samozvanets,
The King, the lords, and Pope support his claim!	Korol' pany i papa za nyevo!

BORIS
(anxiously)

Say what name it is with which he dares to march against me.	Chimzhe imenem na nas on opolchitsa vzdumal?
(rising)	
Come, say what name this wretch usurps . . . What name?	Chyo imya, negodyay, ukral . . .Chyo imya?

SHUISKY
(insinuatingly)

Believe me Tsar, your throne is free from danger.	Konyeshno, tsar, sil'na tvoya derzhava.

(Boris paces the room restlessly.)

Your charity, your kindness and your mercy	Ty milostyu, radyenyem i shchedrotoy
have made you loved by all throughout your realm,	Usynovil serdtsa svoikh rabov,
and every subject is devoted to your throne.	Dushoyu predannykh prestolu tvoyemu.
And as you know most mighty lord and Tsar,	No znaesh sam, veliky gosudar,
it is unwise to depend upon the mob,	Kak lekhko smutit' bessmyslennuyu chern:
for they are obstinate and restless and benighted,	Ona izmyenchiva, myatyezhna, suyevyerna:
and readily are swayed by tales and idle hopes;	Ona vsegda pustoy nadyezhde predana,
the very least suggestion will arouse them;	Malyeyshemu vnusheniyu poslushna,
all of them are weak and blind and superstitious.	K istine prostoy glukha i ravnodushna.
But though it pains me, mighty Tsar, to voice my thoughts,	Khotya i bol'no mnye, veliky gosudar,
although it rends my loyal heart to have to say it,	Khotya i krovyu moyo serdtse obol'yotsa,
I still am bound in truth to tell you . . .	No ot tebya tait' nye smyeyu,

(Boris stands still.)

that if this wretch, who now proclaims himself against you . . .	Shto, yesli, dyerzosti ispolnyenny brodyaga

(Fyodor listens in awe to Shuisky's speech.)

should raise a force and cross into our land,	S Litvy granitsu nashu pereydyot,
the people may well rally to this name:	K nyemu tolpu, byt' mozhet, privlechot
Dimitry, the Tsarevich killed at Uglich! [9]	Dimitriya voskresnuvshee imya!

BORIS
(*starting up*)

Dimitry . . .

Tsarevich, wait outside!

Dimitriya . . .
(*to his son*)
Tsaryevich udalis!

FYODOR

O, my good lord,
consent that I may stay beside you
that I may know the danger that is
threatening Russia's throne.

[18] O gosudar,
Dozvol' mnye pri tebye ostat'sa,
Uznat' bedu, grozyashchuyu prestolu
tvoyemu.

BORIS
(*pacing the room in deep perturbation*)

My child . . .you cannot stay!

Nelzya . . .nelzya, ditya!
(*angrily*)
Tsarevich! Tsarevich! Be obedient!

Tsaryevich! Tsaryevich, povinuysa!

(*Exit Fyodor. Boris follows Fyodor, carefully closing the door behind him, then goes briskly towards Shuisky.*)

Take measures straightaway,
so that the frontier between Poland is
   garrisoned,
so that not a living soul
may cross to violate this land . . .
Now go!

Vzyat' myery, syey zhe chas,
Shtob ob Litvy Rus ogradilas zastavami,

Shtob ni odna dusha
Nye pereshla za etu gran . . .
Stupay! . . .
(*suddenly detaining him*)
No . . .remain, . . .remain, . . .Shuisky!

Nyet!. . .Postoy . . .postoy, Shuysky!
Whoever heard at any time,
of buried children who rise up from their
   coffins
to march against the Tsar, the Tsar
   anointed,
elected by the people
and crowned in the cathedral by the
   patriarch!

Slykhal li ty, kogda-nibud',
Shtob dyeti myortvye iz groba vykhodili . . .

[23] Doprashivat' tsaryey . . .tsaryey zakonnykh,

Izbrannykh vsenarodne,
Uvyenchannykh velikim patriarkhom . . .
(*laughing wildly and grasping Shuisky by the collar*)
What? You frown?
Why aren't you laughing, eh?

Shto? Smeshno?
Shtozh nye smeyoshsa? A?

SHUISKY

Have mercy, most mighty lord and Tsar!

Pomiluy, veliky gosudar!

BORIS

Listen, prince!
Six years ago when that atrocious crime
   was ordered . . .
when that poor child, the royal Prince, met
   his death,
his body lay unburied in the square,
   befouled with bloodstains,
striking pity and wrath in the hearts of
   those who witnessed it
in Uglich, and rousing them to vengeance . . .
Was he who died . . .that infant . . . called
   . . . Dimitry?

Slushay, Knyaz!
Kogda velikoe svershilos zlodeyanye . . .

Kogda bezvryemenno malyutka pogib,

I trup yevo na ploshchadi lezhal
   okrovavlyonny,
Tyazhkoy bolyu v serdtsakh uglichan
   osirotyelikh
Otdavayas i k mshchenyu ikh vzyvaya . . .
Malyutka tot . . . pogibshy . . . byl . . .
   Dimitry?

SHUISKY

Yes!

On!

BORIS

Vassily Ivanych!
By God and by the Cross I now beseech you:
be frank with me! Come let me hear the
   truth;

Vassily Ivanych!
Krestom tebya i bogom zaklinayu,
Po sovesti, vsyu pravdu mnye skazhi,

you know me, I'm merciful.
Your many lies, your former acts of
treason, I can forgive.
But if you try deceit, I swear to you,
I'll order such a fearful death – yes, such
a death
that Tsar Ivan the Terrible will shudder in
his coffin! . . .
Now answer me!

Ty znaesh, ya milostiv:
Proshedshey lzhi opaloyu naprasnoy nye
nakazhu.
No yesli ty skhitrish, klyanus tebye!
Pridumayu ya zluyu kazn, takuyu kazn,

Shto Tsar Ivan ot uzhasa vo grobe
sodrognyotsa! . . .
Otvyeta zhdu!

SHUISKY

You don't believe me, Tsar.
You treat me with mistrust, and doubting
still my loyalty
you threaten punishment and torture.
I fear no death, but only your displeasure!

I ty nye vyerish mnye?
Uzbeli usomnilsa v predannom rabe
tvoyom,
I kaznyu lyutoyu strashchaesh?
Nye kazn strashna, strashna tvoya nemilost'!

(He draws near to Boris, and speaks in a low tone, observing him. The stage is dimly lit.)

In the church at Uglich, before the people,
five days and more, I viewed the body of
the child.
And by his side where thirteen other
corpses
disfigured terribly, their clothing fouled
with bloodstains,
and their flesh, though innocent, showed
traces of corruption.
But all the while the royal child
looked peaceful, pure, and radiant.
All glisteningly, hideously, the wound was
gaping,
yet on his lips so chaste and so guiltless,

V Ugliche, v sobore, pryed vsyem narodom,
Pyat' slishkom dnyey ya trup mladyentsa
naveshchal.
Vokrug nyevo trinadtsat' tyel lezhalo,

Obezobrazhennykh, v krovi, v lokhmotyakh
gryaznykh,
I po nim uzh tlyenie zamyetno prostupalo;

No dyetsky lik tsaryevicha
Byl svyetel, chist i yasen;
Glubokaya, strashnaya ziyala rana;

A na ustakh yevo neporuchnykh

(Boris wipes his face and returns to his chair.)

I saw how wondrously he smiled still;
it seemed the boy who lay there in his cradle
was sound asleep. His arms were folded
and in one hand he grasped a childish toy of
his . . .

Ulybka chudnaya igrala;
Kazalosya v svoyey on kolybyel'ke
Spokoyno spit, slozhivshi ruchki
I v pravoy kryepko szhav igrushku
dyetskuyu . . .

BORIS

Enough, Prince!

Dovol'no! . . .

*(Boris grips the arms of his chair, and waves Shuisky away. Exit Shuisky, watching Boris,
who drops back into his seat.)*

[23]

Ugh! Give me air! I suffocate in here . . .
I felt as if the blood had rushed into my
brain
and slowly then subsided.
Oh, conscience of my soul, how savagely
you punish!

Uf: tyazhelo! Day dukh perevedu . . .
Ya chustvoval vsya krov' mnye kinulas v
litso,
I tyazhko opuskalas.
O, sovest' lyutaya, kak strashno ty
karaesh! . . .

(The stage is in darkness: the clock starts working.)

Now I know if you are stained, but once
are stained,
then nothing can preserve you from
damnation;
your soul will burn, you heart is filled with
poison,
it throbs and throbs within you,
and hammerstrokes ring in your ears with
curses and with hatred . . .
You're choked by something . . . stifled . . .
you feel your head is splitting . . .
and then . . . in blood . . . the murdered
child appears!

Yezheli v tebye pyatno yedinoe . . .

Yedinoe sluchayno zavelosya,

Dusha sgorit, nal' yotsa serdtse yadom,

Tak tyazhko, tyazhko stanet,
Shto molotom stuchit v ushakh ukorom i
proklyatyem . . .
I dushit shto-to . . . dushit . . .
I golova kruzhitsa . . .
V glazakh . . . ditya okrovavlyonnoe! . . .

There . . . just there! . . . What is it? . . . See, it moves! . . .	Von . . . von tam, shto eto . . . tam v uglu . . .
It's quivering . . . it grows . . .	Kolyshetsa, rastyot . . .
it comes to me . . . I hear it groaning . . .	Blizitsa . . . drozhit i stonet . . .
Go . . . Go . . .	Chur, chur . . .
Not I . . . but others were to blame . . .	Nye ya, nye ya tvoy likhodyey . . .
Go, leave me child! . . .	Chur, chur, ditya . . .
Not I . . . not I . . .	Narod . . . nye ya . . .
It was the people! Leave me child!	Volya naroda! . . . Chur, ditya! . . .

(*In terror he hides his face in his hands and falls to his knees by the chair.*)

God above, who desireth not a sinner's death,	Gospodi! ty nye khochesh smyerti gryeshnika,
have mercy on me, and grant my guilty soul forgiveness!	Pomiluy dushu prestupnovo tsarya Borisa!

Curtain.

Richard Van Allan and Fiona Kimm as Boris and Fyodor in the 1980 ENO production by Colin Graham. (photo: Reg Wilson)

Act Three

Scene One. Marina Mniszek's room in the castle of Sandomir. Marina is sitting at her dressing-table; Ruzya dresses her hair, and young girls entertain her with songs.

YOUNG GIRLS*
[24]

By Visla's blue waters, where willows cast shadows,
Stands a fair lily whiter than snowflakes.
Its form is reflected upon the still waters
And idly it gazes, admiring its beauty.

All playful, bewitched by the lily,

A host of gallant butterflies are hovering there around it,
And dazzled by the fair lily's perfection,
Dare not come near the white petals that lure them.

But proudly, half dreaming, the lily ignores them,
And idly it gazes, admiring its beauty.

Na Vislye lazurnoy, pod ivoy tenistoy,
Chudny tsvetochek snega beleye,
V zerkal'nyye vody lenivo glyaditsa,
Lyubuyas svoyey roskoshnoy krasoy.

Nad chudnym tsvetochkom, blistaya na solntse,
Roy babochek rezvykh igraet, kruzhitsa;

Plenyonny divnoy krasoyu tsvetochka,
Nyezhnykh listochkov nye smeyet kosnutsa.

I chudny tsvetochek, kivaya golovkoy,
V zerkal'nyye vody lenivo glyaditsa.

MARINA
(*to her maid*)

My coronet and pearls!

Almazny moy venyets!

YOUNG GIRLS

The Princess Marina, she whom we honour,
Is fairer than lilies, whiter than snowflakes.
Peerless in beauty, unrivalled in sweetness,
The pride and the glory of all Sandomir,
None other can compare.

How many gallants are entranced by her beauty;
They come to pay homage and bow the knee before her,
Imploring, entreating she grants them some favour;
One smile given in answer straightway holds them captive.

But Princess Marina ignores and disdains them.
Their lovesick entreaties, their outbursts of passion,
Their longings, their sorrow, their wistful entreaties
She heeds not.

A v zamkye vesyolom panna krasotka,
Tsvetochka rechnovo krashe, mileye,
Krashe tsvetochka, beleye, nezhneye,
Na slavu i radost' vsyevo Sandomira
Roshkoshno tsvetyot.

Nemalo molodtsev, blestyashchikh i znatnykh,
V nevol' nom smushchenyi pred nyeyu preklonyalis,
Ulybku krasotki blazhenstvom schitaya,

U nog charodyeyki vyes mir zabyvaya.

A panna krasotka lukavo smeyalas

Nad rechyu lyubovnoy, nad strastyu ikh pylkoy
Tomlyenyam i mukam serdyets ikh smushchonnykh
Nye vnemlya.

MARINA
(*to the girls*)

No more, pray!

Dovol'no!
(*rising*)

Your fair Princess is greatly honoured
to hear you sing her praises,
and thanks you for comparing her
to that same lily white as snowflakes.

Krasotka panna blagodarna,
Za laskovoye slovo i sravnyenye
S tyem tsvetochkom chudnym,
Shto beleye snyega.

---

* *The song of the Young Girls was originally written in short lines, two of which make up the lines as laid out here.*

And yet Marina takes no pleasure
in empty adulation
or absurd allusions to those
idle gallants sick with amorous passion.
No more of foolish lovers who dance
    attendance on her,
and fondly sigh and languish!
Songs like these that tell my praise can
    never please me;
Princess Mniszek merely scorns such words
    that flatter!
Sing instead those famous ballads which
I've loved since days of childhood,
songs of heroes brave in battle,
songs of Poland's martial glory!
Songs of valiant warrior maidens
songs of Poland's conquered foemen . . .
This is what delights Marina;
noble songs like these inspire her.

(to the girls)

Now leave me!

No panna Mnishek nedovol'na
Ni rechyu vashey l'stivoy
Ni bessmyslennym namyokom
Na kakikh-to molodtsev blistyashchikh
Shto tseloyu tolpoyu u nog yeyo lezhali,

V blazhenstvye utopaya.
Nyet, nye etikh pyesen nuzhno pannye
    Mnishek;
Nye pokhval krasye svoyey ot vas zhdala ya.

A tyekh pyesenok chudyesnykh,
Shto mnye nyanya napevala:
O velichyi, o pobyedakh
I o slavye boyev pol'skikh,
O vsemoshchnykh pol'skikh dyevakh,
O pobitykh inozemtsakh.
Vot shto nuzhno pannye Mnishek,
Eti pyesni yey otrada.

Stupayte.

(The girls curtsey and leave. To Ruzya.)

Leave me, I do not need you, Ruzya;
go and rest.

Ty, Ruzya, mnye nye nuzhna sevodnya;
Otdokhni.

(Exit Ruzya.)

Ah, life is tedious! Yes, so tedious!
Oh, these days that pass so slowly,
days of endless tedium,
empty, wearisome, and barren!
Neither courtiers versed in charm,
nor crowds of foolish suitors,
can dispel my constant boredom.
And yet, amid the gloom,
a welcome star shines out to cheer me;
that gallant who claims the Russian
throne has caught Marina's fancy.
My Dimitry, strong and fearless,
unrelenting,
sent by God to render justice,
you'll avenge the young Tsarevich,
put to death through lust for power.
At your hand that foul usurper,
Boris, will meet with retribution.
I shall rouse the Polish nobles.
Lured by gold and dreams of glory
they shall all obey me!
As for you, my own Dimitry,
shy and tender lover,
I shall melt your heart
with tears of burning passion.
In my arms I'll then embrace you,
smother you with kisses,
my Tsarevich, my Dimitry,
my predestined bridegroom.
I shall charm your every sense
with words of loving ardour.
Not for me the joys of hearing
sighs of unrequited passion,
solemn vows from callow suitors,
empty boasts of pompous nobles.
Princess Mniszek longs for glory,
Princess Mniszek thirsts for power!
I shall sit as your Tsaritsa
on the throne of Russia,
clothed in robe of gold and purple,

Skuchno Marinye, akh, kak skuchno!
[25] Kak tomitel'no i vyalo
Dni za dnyami dlyatsa.
Pusto, glupo tak, besplodno;
Tsely sonm knyazyey i grafov.
I panov vel'mozhnykh
Nye razgonit skuki adskoy.
Lish tam, v tumannoy dali,
Zorka yasnaya blesnula;
To Moskovsky prokhodimets
Pannye Mnishek priglyanulsa.
Moy Dimitriy, mstitel' grozny,
Besposhchadny,
Bozhy sud, i bozhya kara
Za tsaryevicha malyutku,
Zhertvu vlasti nenasytnoy,
Zhertvu alchnosti i zloby
Tsarya zlodyeya, Godunova.
Razbuzhu magnatov sonnykh,
Blyeskom zlata i dobychi
Zamanyu ya shlyakhtu.
A tebya, moy samozvanets,
Moy lyubovnik tomny,
Opoyu tebya slezami
Strasti zhguchey
Zadushu tebya v obyatyakh,
Zatseluyu mily
Moy tsaryevich, moy Dimitriy,
Moy zhenikh nazvany
Nyezhnym lyepetom lyubovnym
Slukh tvoy ocharuyu.
Pannye Mnishek slishkom skuchny:
Strasti tomnoy izliyanya,
Pylkikh yunoshey molyenya,
Rechni poshlyye magnatov.
Panna Mnishek slavy khochet,
Panna Mnishek vlasti zhazhdet!
Na prestol tsaryey moskovskikh
Ya tsaritsey syadu,
I, v porfirye zlatotkannoy,

like the sun in splendour!	Solntsem zablistayu.
With my beauty I shall dazzle	A krasoyu svoyey chudyesnoy
all the stupid folk of Moscow;	Ya srazhu tupykh moskalyey,
I shall curb the haughty boyars,	I stado boyar kichlivykh
make them kneel to me in homage.	Bit' chelom sebye zastavlyu.
And the people then shall	I proslavyat v skazkakh,
praise their proud Tsaritsa:	Bylyakh nebylitsakh
song and legend shall extol me,	Gorduyu svoyu tsaritsu
all shall fear Marina Mniszek!	Tupoumnyye moskali!
Ha, ha, ha!	Kha, kha, kha!

(*Laughing aloud, she goes towards the door, stopping before a mirror, to admire herself and adjust her coronet. She sees reflected in it the Jesuit, who is standing humbly at the door, and cries out.*)

| Oh! Ah! It is you, holy father! | A! Akh, eto ty, moy otyets! |

RANGONI

With dutiful respect before such radiant beauty,	Dozvolit li nichtozhnomu rabu gospodnyu
the Lord's most humble slave presents himself before you,	Krasoyu nezemnoy blistayushchaya panna
and begs to speak with you.	Prosit' vnimaniya.

(*He bows.*)

MARINA

My father, you have no need to ask.	Otyets moy, vy nye prosit' dolzhny
Marina Mniszek ever since a child has	Marina Mnishek docheryu poslushnoyu
always been and will be	Byla i budyet
a faithful daughter of the Catholic religion.	Svyatoy apostol'skoy nerazdyel'noy tserkvi.

RANGONI

| Our Church, alas, has been abandoned and forgotten. | [26] Tserkov bozhya ostavlyena, zabyta |

(*coming closer to Marina*)

The holy icons of our saints have faded;	Liki svyelyye svyatykh poblyekli,
dogma and faith have lost their power to guide us,	Vyery zhivoy istochnik chisty glokhnyet,
yea, the smouldering censers burn but feebly.	Ogn kadil'nits blagovonnykh myerknet,
The wounds of martyrs are bleeding in anguish,	Ziyayut rany svyatykh strastotyerptsev,
shrines and convents lie desolate, empty.	Skorb i stony v obitelyakh gornikh,
God's own angels weep in lamentation!	Lyutsa slyozy pastyryey smiryennykh.

MARINA

My father, you . . .you have filled me with distress.	Otyets moy! vy . . .vy smushchaete menya.
Burning sympathy, stirred by our Church's plight,	Bolyu zhgucheyu rech vasha skorbnaya
wakes within my conscience and my spirit.	V slabom moyom syerdtse otdayotsa.

RANGONI

Dearest child! Marina!	Doch moya! Marina!
You must convert the faithless crowds of Moscow!	Provozvesti yeretikam-moskalyam
Teach our faith to them;	Vyeru pravuyu
guide their steps on the path of salvation;	Obrati ikh na put' spasyenya,
crush their spirit of sinful dissension.	Sokrushi dukh raskola grekhovny,
And the grace of our Lord will reward you;	I proslavyat Marinu svyatuyu
yea, his angels will pray for your soul	Pred prestolom tvortsa lulhezarnym
and glorify Marina!	Angely gospodni.

MARINA
(*rejoicing at the thought*)

And the grace of our Lord will reward me,	I proslavyat Marinu svyatuyu
all his angels will pray for my soul	Pred prestolom tvortsa luchezarnym
and glorify Marina!	Angely gospodni!

(coming to her senses)

Oh, sinful pride!	U! grekh kakoy!
My father, with what enticements	Otyets moy, soblaznom strashnym
you try to lure and tempt the sinful soul	Vy iskusili dushu greshnuyu
of ignorant and frivolous Marina!	Neopytnoy i vyetrennoy Mariny.
Not I, who thirst for glory,	Nye mnye, privykshey k blyesku,
I who revel in the world of pleasure,	V vikhre svyeta i pirov vesyolykh,
am the one whom God has chosen	Nyet, nye mnye na dolyu palo
to lead his Church to glory:	Proslavit' tserkov bozhyu.
I am helpless . . .	Ya bessil'na.

RANGONI

Your beauty must serve to bewitch the Pretender!	[27] Krasoyu svoyeyu pleni samozvantsa!
Lure him with words full of amorous promises,	[28] Rechyu lyubovnoyu, nyezhnoyu, pylkoyu,
words that will rouse him to passion:	Strasti zaroni v yevo syerdtse.
look at him tenderly, smile at him lovingly,	Plamennym vzorom, ulybkoy charuyushchey.
make him your dutiful slave.	Razum yevo pokori.
Ignore any maidenly stirrings of conscience,	Prezri, suyevyerny, nelyepy strakh
despise all timorous scruples.	Ugryzyeniy sovyesti zhalkoy,
Scorn superstition and bigoted prejudice,	Bros predrasudok, pusoy i zabavny,
banish all shyness, and modest pretences!	Devichey stydlivosti, lozhnoy i vzdornoy.
At times pretend to be angry,	Poroyu gnyevom pritvornym,
resort to caprice and deception.	Kapriznoyu prikhotyu zhenskoy,
At others yield to his pleading, inflame him with passion . . .	Poroyu tonkoyu lyestyu, il' lovkim obmanon
Make him yearn for you, make him pine for you . . .	Iskusi yevo, obol'sti yevo.
Then, when helpless with love he completely surrenders,	I kogda istomlyonny, u nog tvoikh divnykh,
and stands at your mercy, awaiting your orders:	V vostorgye bezmolvnom, zhdat' budyet velyeniy,
force him to swear full allegiance to Rome!	Klyatvu potrebuy svyatoy propagandy!

MARINA
(reluctantly)

And why should I do this?	Tovo li mnye nuzhno!

RANGONI
(severely)

What? You dare oppose me,	Kak? I ty derzaesh
and defy your religion!	Protivitsa tserkvi!
Love for your church demands that you serve her,	Yesli za blago priznano budyet,
and sacrifice all that you cherish	Dolzhna ty pozhertvovat' totchas,
in humble, willing obedience,	Bez strakha, bez sozhalyenya,
your honour if need be!	Chestyu svoyeyu!

MARINA
(angrily)

Stop, wretched serf!	Shto? dyerzky Izhets!
You Jesuit sunk in depravity,	Klyanu tvoi rechi lukavyye,
no more of your devilish sophistry!	Syerdtse tvoyo razvrashchonnoye,
I curse you, I loathe and despise you.	Klyanu tebya vsyey siloy prezreniya.
Go, leave my sight!	Proch s glaz moikh!

RANGONI
(going towards the door)

Marina!	Marina!

(returning to her gradually)

Terrible flames seem to blaze from your eyes as in frenzy.	Plamenem adskim glaza tvoi zasverkali,
Your lips are distorted, your cheeks are bloodless;	Usta iskazilis, shchoki poblyekli;

| a blast of foulest impurity has withered your loveliness. | Ot dunovyenya nechistovo ischezla krasa tvoya. |

MARINA
(in superstitious terror)

| Protect me, spare my soul, O Lord! Save me, show me mercy, Lord! | O bozhe, zashchiti menya! Nauchi menya! |

RANGONI

| Powers of hell confound and deceive you, your pride is inspired by the spirit of evil. | Dukhi t'my toboy ovladyeli, Gordynyey besovskoy tvoy um omrachili, |

(coming closer)

| Spreading his wings in his fearful triumph Satan himself is standing above you . . . | V groznom velichyi, na krylyakh adskikh, Sam satana parit nad toboyu! |

MARINA
(falling at his feet with a loud cry)

| Ah! | A! |

RANGONI
(as if he were crouching over his prey) [27]

| Obey the envoy of God. You must submit, soul and body, submit your inmost feelings and ambitions, and be henceforth my slave! | Smiris pred bozhyim poslom! Predaysya mnye vsyey dushoyu, Vsyem pomyslom, zhelanyem i mechtoyu; Moyeyu bud' raboy! |

Curtain.

Scene Two. *The garden of the Mniszek Castle of Sandomir. A fountain in the moonlight.*

DIMITRY
(coming out of the castle, lost in thought) [9]

| Midnight . . . the grove . . . by the fountain . . . O voice of wonder! Your words enchant me and fill my heart with rapture! | V polnich . . . v sadu . . . u fontana, O golos divny! Kakoy otradoy ty mnye napolnil syerdtse! |

(approaching the fountain)

| Beloved, will you come to me, or do I but wait in the darkness in vain for you? Have you forgotten your faithful Dimitry who yearns and languishes sick with love for you? One word of sympathy, just one smile from you and you will ease all the anguish that I feel for you. | Pridyosh li ty, zhelannaya, Pridyosh li, golubka moya lyokhko-krylaya? Al' nye vspomyanyesh ty buynovo sokola Shto po tebye grustit, nadryvaetsa? Privyetom laskovym, rechyu nyezhnoyu Ty utoli muku syerdtsa bezyskhodnuyu. |

(turning towards the castle)

| Marina! Marina! | Marina! Marina! |

(walking towards the castle)

| Oh, answer! Do but answer! I wait, I wait and long for you! No, all is silent! | Otkliknis, o, otkliknis! Pridi, pridi, ya zhdu tebya! Nyet, nyet otvyeta. |

(He is lost in thought. Around a corner of the wall appears the Jesuit, proceeding cautiously and looking around him.) [27]

RANGONI

| Tsarevich! | Tsaryevich! |

DIMITRY

| What, you again! Your shadow haunts me day and night. | Opyat' za mnoy! Kak tyen preslyeduesh menya. |

Most brave, illustrious Tsarevich!	Svetlyeyshy, doblestny tsaryevich!
I come to you,	Ya poslan k vam
sent by the proud and beautiful Marina —	Gordoyu krasavitsey Marinoy ...

DIMITRY

Marina!	Marinoy?

RANGONI

That dear obedient child	Poslushnoy, nyezhnoy docheryu,
whom Heaven entrusts to my keeping.	Mnye nyebom vruchonnoy.
She begged me to find you and tell you	Ona umolyala skazat' vam,
what spiteful and slanderous rumours	Shto mnogo nasmyeshek zlobnykh
she suffers for your sake.	Prishlos perenyat' yey,
How dearly she loves you and longs for you ...	Shto vas ona lyubit, shto budyet k vam ...

DIMITRY

Oh, if you do not lie,	O, yesli ty nye lzhozh,
if no spirit from hell	Yesli nye sam Satana
whispers these wonderful words to me ...	Shepchet tye rechi chudyesnyye ...
then I swear to raise my beloved	Voznesu yeyo, golubku,
above all women on earth!	Pred vsyeyu russkoy zemlyoy,
I shall lead her soon to Moscow, to reign by my side,	Vozvedu yeyo s soboyu na tsarsky prestol,
she shall dazzle with her beauty all the Russian folk!	Osleplyu yeyo krasoyu pravoslavny lyud!

(watching the Jesuit)

Vile tempter!	Zloy dyemon!
Like a thief at night you came to surprise me,	Ty, kak tat' nochnoy, zakralsa mnye v dushu,
intending to expose my inmost feelings;	Ty vyrval iz grudi moyey priznanye ...
say, were those words of love not lies?	Ty o lyubvi Mariny lgal?

RANGONI

Lies? I lie? Could I lie to you, Tsarevich?	Lgal? ya lgal? I pyered toboy, tsaryevich?
It is for you alone that day and night	Da po tebye odnom i dyen, i noch
the love-sick Marina yearns and suffers,	Ona tomitsa i stradaet,
as she sits alone in silence	O, sud'be tvoyey zavidnoy
and dreams of your future glory.	V nochnoy tishi mechtaet:
Oh, if you only loved her,	O, yeslib ty lyubil yeyo,
if you but knew how much she suffers:	Yesliby znal yeyo terzanya
how all the courtiers mock her:	Gordykh panov nasmyeshki,
how envious women accuse her,	Zavist' ikh zhon litsemyernykh,
spitefully gossip, talk of you meeeting	Poshlyye splyetni, bredni pustyye,
at night in the garden,	O taynykh svidanyakh,
spread lying rumours,	O posteluyakh,
whisper aloud their scurrilous insults ...	Roy oskorblyeniy nevynosimikh ...
Oh, then you would not disregard	O, ty nye otvyerg by togda
my eager entreaties, and truthful assurance,	Mol'by moyey skromnoy, moikh uveryeniy,
or disbelieve the distress of suffering Marina.	Lozhyu nye nazval by muku byednoy Mariny.

DIMITRY

No more pray! Stop these bitter reproaches!	Dovol'no! Slishkom mnogo upryokov,
Far too long have I hidden from the world	Slishkom dolgo skryval ya to lyudyey
that I love her.	Svoyo schastye!

(with great determination)

No longer shall Marina suffer;	Ya za Marinu grudyu stanu,
I'll take revenge on all those nobles,	Ya doproshu panov nadmyennykh,
I'll stop the tongues of those envious women ...	Kovarsvo zhon ikh besstydynykh razrushu.
I'll hold them up to shame and derision,	Ya osmyeyu ikh zhalkuyu zlobu,
I'll face those despicable princes and lordlings	Pred tseloy tolpoyu bezdushnykh panyenok

and boldly proclaim my great love for Marina, | Otkroyus v lyubvi bezgranichnoy Marinye,

(fervently)

then fall at her feet and ardently beg her not to reject my devotion to her, but be my Tsaritsa, my well-beloved treasure! | Ya broshus k nogam yeyo, umolyaya Nye otvergat' pylkoy strasti moyey, Byt' mnye zhenoyu, tsaritsey, drugom.

RANGONI
(aside)

May Saint Ignatius aid my purpose! | Vspomoshchestvuy, svyatoy Ignatiy!

DIMITRY
(to Rangoni)

You, who scorn all earthly weakness, who swore to renounce the joys mortals delight in; you for whom love and its wiles have no secrets, I adjure you now, by all the vows you have sworn, yes, by the strength of your hope in salvation! | Ty, otryokshysya ot mira, Proklyatyu predvashy vsye radosti zhizni, Master veliky v lyubovnom iskusstvye, Zaklinayu tebya, vsyey siloy klyatvy tvoyey, Vsyey siloy zhazhdy blazhenstva nebyesnovo!

Now lead me to her, oh, let me see her at once, let me speak of the love I feel, and my longing for her: then name me your price, and I'll pay you forthwith! | Vedi menya k nyey, o day uvidet' yeyo, Day skazat' o lyubvi moyey, o stradanyakh moikh, I nyet toy tseny, shto smutila b menya!

RANGONI

Tsarevich, I am but a priest, a servant of God, I spend my time in thoughts of what's to come upon the dread day of Judgment, when man shall receive his just reward or punishment; I live in dim seclusion, free from envy. What have I to do with earthly riches? And yet if Dimitry would do God's bidding and consider my humble petition, let me stand close by him as a father, and follow his every footstep, thought and purpose, guide him and shelter him ... | Smirenny, greshny bogomolyets Za blizhnikh svoikh, O strashnom dnye poslyednevo suda, O groznoy karye gospodney, Gryadushchey v tot dyen, Vsechasno pomyshlyayushchy, Trup, davno otzhivshy, khladny kamen, Mozhet li zhelat' sokrovishch zhizni! No yesli Dimitriy vnushenyem bozhyim, Nye otvergnyet zhelaniy smirennykh Nye pokidat' yevo kak syna, Sledit' za kazhdym shagom yevo i myslyu, Berech i okhranyat' yevo ...

DIMITRY

Why, then it shall be as you wish if you take me at once to Marina, my love, my paragon ... | Da, ya nye rasstanus s toboy, Tol'ko day mnye uvidet' Marinu moyu, Obnyat' yeyo.

RANGONI

Tsarevich, hide now! | Tsaryevich, skryoysa!

DIMITRY

Why should I? | Shto s toboy?

RANGONI

The crowd of noble guests will see you waiting in the garden. Away, Tsarevich, I implore you, away! | Tebya zastanyet zdes Tolpa piruyushchikh magnatov. Uydi, tsaryevich, umolyayu, uydi!

DIMITRY

Let them come, for here I am remaining to greet each one as he deserves ... | Pust' idut, ya vstrechu ikh s pochotom, Po sanu, doblesti i chesti.

Be careful, Tsarevich, you will ruin yourself	Opomnis, tsaryevich, ty pogubish sebya
and ruin Marina: away I tell you!	Ty vidash Marinu, uydi skoreye!

He forces Dimitry to leave. Exeunt. From the castle, down the balcony steps, enter a crowd of guests, headed by Marina on the arm of an old nobleman. The guests cross the stage in couples and disappear into the garden. / Polonaise [29]

MARINA

How can I believe you love me, Marquis?	Vashey strasti ya nye vyeryu, panye,
All your vows and protestations fail to move me.	Vashey klyatvy, uverenya, vsyo naprasno!
Do not think that I will trust them ...	I nye mozhete vy, panye ...

(They go off into the garden.)

GUESTS

Soon our troops will overthrow the Russian kingdom!	I Moskovsko tsarstvo my polonim zhivo!
We shall bring our captives home to you, fair ladies!	I moskalyey plyennykh privedyom k vam, panni!
Tsar Boris and all his army shall surrender!	A voyska Borisa razobyom navyerno!
Then delay no further, lose no time in starting ...	Nu, tak shto zhe, panye shto myedlit, pany?
Go to Moscow, take the city,	Na Moskvu skorey idite
bring back Tsar Boris as captive ...	I Borisa v plyen berite ...

(They go into the garden, then return and start to re-enter the castle.)

For Poland's fame and glory,	Dlya Rechi Pospolitoy
we must overthrow the power of Russia!	Nuzhno razorit' gnezdo moskalyey!
Marina knows no better ...	Marina nye sumeyet.
she's lovely but so cold ... her heart's like ice ...	Kraziva, no sukha, nadmyenna, zla.

MARINA

(from the balcony, about to enter the castle)

Some wine, some wine, my friends!	Vina, vina, panovye!

GUESTS

A toast to fair Marina!	Da zdravstvuyet Marina!

(All follow Marina into the castle.)

Toast, my lords, the house of Mniszek!	Pyom bokal vo zdravye Mnishkov!
A health unto our lovely hostess!	Vengyerskim chestvovat' Marinu!
Marina soon shall wear the crown of Russia!	Vo slavu tsarskovo ventsa Mariny!

(off-stage)

Vivat, vivat, vivat!	Vivat, vivat, vivat!

DIMITRY

(rushing in, shaking himself)

Oh, that crafty Jesuit! How he clung to me	Iezuit lukavy krepko szhal menya
and gripped me with his talons!	V kogtyakh svoikh proklyatikh.
For one brief moment, fleetingly, I caught	Ya tol'ko melkom, izdali, uspel,
a glimpse of beautiful Marina,	Vzglyanut' na divnuyu Marinu,
and secretly, in silent rapturous delight,	Ukradkoy vstretit' blyesk charuyushchikh
beheld her radiance.	Ochey yeyo chudyesnykh.
But my poor heart was beating,	A syerdtse bilos sil'no,
beating so wildly,	Tak sil'no bilos.
that I longed to push aside the sly Rangoni,	Shto nye raz tolkalo s boya vzyat' svobodu,
shake off the clutching fingers of the Jesuit,	Podratsa s pokrovitelyem nezvannym,
the guardian of my conscience!	Otsom moim dukhovnym!
And while he talked and whispered there his pack of lies	Pod boltovnyu nesnosnuyu yevo rechey,
and traded on my secret,	Do naglosti lukavykh,
I saw Marina, my adored Tsaritsa,	Ya videl pod ruku s panom bezzubym,
go past upon the arm of some rich dotard!	Nadmyennuyu krasavitsu Marinu:
She whispered in his ear and smiled so sweetly!	Plenitel'noy ulybkoyu siyaya,

No doubt she spoke with feeling of love's
  enchantments,
of secret passion, of the joys of holy
  wedlock . . .
the wife of some profligate old dandy!
When fortune offers her
the delights of love and dominion,
a kingdom and the throne of mighty
  Russia! . . .
No, God forbid!
Without delay I'll don my armour,
my shield and trusty helmet,
and then to horse! Ahead!
To death or glory!
Proudly I'll ride before my brave warriors.
Boldly we'll face the foe, bring him to bay,
claiming my heritage, the throne of the
  Tsars!

Prelestnitsa sheptala o laskye nyezhnoy,

O strasti tikhoy, o schastyi byt' suprugoy . . .

Suprugoy bezzubovo kutily!
Kogda sud'ba sulit yey
Lyubvi blazhenstva i slavu;
Venyets zlatoy tsarskoyu porfiru!

Nyet, k chortu vsyo!
Skoreye v brannyye dospyekhi!
Shelom i myech bulatny,
I na konyey! Vperyod!
Na symertny boy!
Mchatsa v glavye druzhiny khorobroy,
Vstretit! litsom k litsu vrazhyi polki,
S boya, so slavoy, vzyat' naslyedny prestol!

(Enter Marina.)

MARINA

Dimitry! Tsarevich Dimitry!

Dimitriy! Tsaryevich Dimitriy!

DIMITRY
(appearing from among the trees)

At last, Marina!

Ona! Marina!

(He hurries towards her.)

Yes, it's you, beloved,
enchantress of my heart!
Ah, how wearily, how slowly,
time seemed to pass as I stood waiting,
filling my heart with fearful suffering.
Torments of doubt excited my jealousy
  there in the darkness,
and turned each new avowal of my love
  into curses.

Zdes, moya golubka,
Krasavitsa moya.
[30] Kak tomitel'no, kak dolgo,
Dlilis minuty ozhidanya
Skol'ko muchitel'nykh somnyeniy,
Syerdtse terzaya, svyetlyye dumy moi
  omrachali,
Lyubov moyu i schastye proklinat'
  zastavlyali.

MARINA

I know, you're lovesick!
You cannot sleep, you dream all day
as heart and soul are both consumed
by love for Marina.
I did not come this evening
to hear your amorous protestations,
for I'm tired of them.
When you're alone at leisure,
you then may suffer as you please
and pine for me.

Znayu, vsyo znayu!
Nochey nye spish, mechtaesh ty,
I dyen i noch mechtaesh
I svoyey Marinye.
Nye dlya besyed lyudovnykh,
Nye dlya rechey pustykh i vzdornykh
Ya prishla k tebye.
Nayedinye s soboyu
Ty mozhesh mlyet' i tayat'
Ot lyubvi ko mnye.

DIMITRY

Marina!

Marina?

MARINA

I'm not the least impressed if for my sake
you languish or even die for me
because you love me so!
How soon will you reign in Moscow as the
  Tsar?

Menya nye udivyat, ty dolzhen znat'
No zhertvy, ni dazhe smyert' tvoya
Iz-za lyubvi ko mnye.
Kogda zh tsaryom ty budyesh v Moskvye?

DIMITRY

As Tsar? Marina, how your words distress
  me!
Must I believe that shallow lure of power,
the intrigues of the court, its calumnies and
  slanders,

Tsaryom? Marina, ty pugaesh syerdtse!

Uzheli vlast', siyaniye prestola,
Kholopov podlykh roy, ikh gnusnyye
  donosy

could quench within your eager soul
the sacred longing for passion's ardour,
for heartfelt love and affection, for fond
  embraces
and the magic enchantment of the ecstasy
  of passion?

V tebye mogli by zadushit'
Svyatuyu zhazhdu lyubvi vzaimnoy,
Otradu laski serdyechnoy, obyatiy zharkikh;

I strastnykh vostorgov charuyushchuyu
  silu!

MARINA
(ironically)

Of course not!
All I want is some poor cottage
where we both could live alone.
What is glory, what's a kingdom?
Love's enchantment far outweighs a
  throne!
Should it be, Tsarevich, that only love
  concerns you,
then make your choice at home, among all
  your Russian women.
They're lovely, voluptuous, tender, and
  passionate!

Konyeshno!
My i v khizinye ubogoy
Budyem schastlivy s toboy;
Shto nam slava, shto nam tsarstvo?
My lyubovyu budyem zhit' odnoy!

Yesli vy, tsaryevich, odnoy lyubvi khotite,

V Moskovii u vas naydyotsa nemalo
  zhenshchin,
Debyelykh, rumyanykh, brov sobolinaya.

DIMITRY

Oh! Do not talk of them!
They only care about their
life of easy luxury!
Just speak one word to them of love,
and they will straightway fawn upon you!
It's you, yes, you alone, Marina,
You who I worship, you are my passion,
you are my hope and my salvation.
Pity the anguish that racks this aching
  heart of mine . . .
Ah, do not turn from me!

Shto nashi zhenshchiny!
V pukhovikakh valyatsa,
Mlet' i tayat', lyubo im!
Shepni khot' slovo o lyubvi,
Raskisnut tak, shto toshno stanyet!
Tebya, tebya odnu, Marina,
Ya obozhayu, vsyey siloy strasti,
Vsyey zhazhdoy nyegi i blazhenstva,
Zhal'sa nad skorbyu isterzannoy dushi
  moyey
Nye otvergay menya!

MARINA

It is not I, then,
only my beauty that attracts you to me!
I desire the throne of Russia,
robes of purple and a diadem . . .
Only these might tempt Marina!

Tak nye Marinu,
Vo tol'ko zhenshchinu vo mnye lyubili?
Lish prestol tsarey moskovskikh,
Lish porfira i venyets zlatoy
Iskusit' menya mogli by.

DIMITRY

Your bitter taunts will break my heart,
  unkind Marina!
My blood runs cold to hear your words of
  cold rejection.
Say that you would love me still,
yes, even were I not the Tsar,
do not despise this love that tortures and
  burns me!

Ty ranish syerdtse mnye, zhestokaya
  Marina,
Ot slov tvoikh mogil'ny khlad na dushu
  vyeyet.
Vidish, ya u nog tvoikh, u nog tvoikh
  molyu tebya;
Nye otvergay lyubvi moyey bezumnoy!

MARINA
(pushing Dimitry away with her foot) [31]

Rise, my timid suitor,
do not tire yourself with idle pleading.
Rise, my lovesick martyr:
I pity you, my angel.
You're exhausted, weak, and helpless,
faint with love for fair Marina.
Day and night you're lost in dreaming,
and quite forget your throne in Moscow,
and the Tsar you mean to conquer . . .
Go, you brazen upstart!

Vstan', lyubovnik nyezhny.
Nye tomi sebya mol'boy naprasnoy,
Vstan', stradalyets tomny!
Mnye zhal' tebya, moy mily.
Iznemog ty, istomilsa
Ot lyubvi k svoyey Marinye,
Dyen i noch o nyey mechtaesh,
Zabyl i dumat' o prestolye,
O borbye s tsaryom Borisom
Proch, brodyaga derzky!

DIMITRY

Marina! Pity me!   Marina, shto s toboy?

MARINA

Go, you fawning minion . . .   Proch, prispyeshnik pansky!

DIMITRY

Pity me!   Shto s toboy?

MARINA

You serf!   Kholop!

DIMITRY

Stop, Marina!   Stoy, Marina!
I see that you are trying to revile   Mnye chudilos, ty brosila
and taunt me for the life I've left behind   Ukorom tyagostnym moyey minuvshey
  me . . .   zhizni.
You lie, proud and haughty Princess;   Lzhosh, gordaya polyachka! Tsaryevich ya!
  Dimitry speaks!
From every end of Russia's mighty empire, [9]   So vsyekh kontsov Rusi vozhdi steklisya,
I'll summon warriors to lead me on to   Zautra v boy letim v glavye druzhin
  victory.   khorobrykh,
All shall witness us marching on the   Slavnym vityazem pryamo v kreml'
  Kremlin;   Moskovsky,
the throne of the Tsars awaits its rightful   Na otchiy prestol, zavyeshchany sud'boy.
  heir!
But when I am Tsar in Moscow and sit in   No kogda tsaryom ya syadu, v velichyi
  regal splendour,   nepristupnom,
Oh, with what delight I'll show my con-   O s kakim vostorgom ya nasmeyus nad
  tempt for you then!   toboy,
Oh, with what joy I'll take my revenge   O kak okhotno ya posmotryu na tebya,
  upon you;
as you will kneel at my footstool and beg my   Kak ty, potyeryannym tsarstvom terzayas,
forgiveness and curse yourself, bitterly   Raboyu polushnoyu, budyesh poltzti
  grieving
over the kingdom you have lost.   K podnozhyu prestola moyevo
Everyone will treat you with contempt   Vsyem togda smeyatsa ya velyu
and laughingly deride you.   Nad duroyu-shlyakhtyankoy!

MARINA

Deride me!   Smeyatsa!
O Tsarevich, I implore you,   [32] O tsaryevich, umolyayu,
do not take to heart the foolish words that I   Nye klyani menya za rechi zlyye moi,
  spoke,
for I love you, I adore you, and spoke but to   Nye ukorom, nye nasmyeshkoy, no
  wake in you   chistoy lyubovyu,
pride in honour and fame, pride in your   Zhazhdoy slavy tvoyey, zhazhdoy velichya,
  glory!
My heart and soul are yours always,   Zvuchat oni v tishi nochnoy
my darling, my precious one.   Moy mily, kokhany moy,
For your loving Marina could not deceive   Nye izmenit tebye tvoya Marina!
  you.
Forget, yes, forget   Zabud' zabud' o nyey,
that she worships you,   Zabud' o lyubvi svoyey,
and hasten to conquer your throne!   Skoreye na tsarsky prestol!

DIMITRY

Marina!   Marina!
Think how I suffer for love of you!   Adskuyu muku dushi moyey
Do not torment me with further falsehood.   Nye rastravlay lyubovyu pritvornoy!

MARINA

I love you, my Dimitry;   Lyublyu tebya, moy kokhany,
My lord and master!   Moy povelitel'!

DIMITRY

Oh, say those words yet again, Marina!	O, povtori, povtori, Marina!
Let my suffering heart find contentment;	O, nye day ostyt' naslazhdyenyu,
fill my soul with rapture, my heavenly enchantress,	Day dushe otradu, moya charovnitsa
paragon!	Zhizn' moya!

MARINA
(kneeling)

Hail Tsar!	Tsar moy!

DIMITRY

Rise, my wonderful, peerless Tsaritsa!	Vstan' tsaritsa moya, nenaglyadnaya!
Rise, let me hold and cherish you!	Vstan' obnimi zhelannovo!

MARINA

Ah, my heart is revived by my hero,	O, kak syerdtse moyo ozhivil ty,
by my conqueror.	Povelitel' moy!

(They kiss. Rangoni, crossing the stage, stops to watch the lovers kissing, and rejoices at this proof of his victory.)

RANGONI
(at a distance) [27]

Oo! Amorous turtle-doves,	O, golubki moi!
you are so simple, so credulous!	O. kak vy prosty, kak nyezhny!
Loving glances, ardent embraces,	S tomnym vzorom, v zharkikh obyatyakh,
and I at last have gained my end!	Dobycha vyernaya moya!

MARINA

O my Dimitry!	O, moy Dimitriy!
Think of your armies that wait:	Voysko davno zhdyot tebya,
prepare to march and conquer your throne.	Speshi v Moskvu, na tsarsky prestol!

DIMITRY

Sweetest Marina!	Moya Marina!
Soon you and I will be united,	Skoro l' blazhenstva mig nastanyet,
yes, the dawn of our happiness draws near!	Skoro l' schastya zhelanny dyen pridyot!

Curtain.

Marina (Josephine Veasey) spurns Dimitry (William McAlpine) at Covent Garden in 1974.
(photo: Donald Southern)

93

Act Four

(*Initial Version*)

A square in front of the Cathedral of Basil the Blessed in Moscow. A crowd of poor people wander aimlessly about. Women are seated apart by the side-door of the Cathedral. Police Officers appear now and then among the crowd. A group of men, headed by Mityukha, enter from the Cathedral.

MEN
(*talking among themselves*)

What, has the service finished?	Shto, otoshla obyedyna?
Yes! And he was cursed once again.	Da, uzh proklinali tovo.
But who is he?	Kovo eto?
That Grishka boy,	A Grishka-to,
Grishka Otrepiev.	Grishku Otryepyeva.
Fancy!	Vot shto.

MITYUKHA

Out among them comes the deacon,	Vyshel eto, bratsy, dyakon
that great big one, that fat one,	Zdorovyenny, da tolsty,
and he shouted:	Da kak garknyet:
"Grishka Otrepiev, anathema!"	"Grishka Otryepyev — anafyema!"

MEN

That's nonsense! You're just joking!	Chevo, chort! shto ty bryeshesh?
Or else you've lost your senses.	Al' byeleny ob'yelsa.
It's true we tell you!	Vzapravdu, bratsy!
That's exactly what he said:	Vot tak-taki khvatil:
"Grishka Otrepiev," he declared, "anathema!"	Grishka Otryepyev, govorit, anafyema!
Ha, ha, ha, well, let him.	Kha, kha, kha, da nu ikh!
Let Grishka be accursed;	Tsaryevichu plevat',
what's that to our Tsarevich!	Shto Grishku proklinayut.
Can he be Grishka?	Neshto na Grishka!
It's certain.	Vestimo!

MITYUKHA

But they sang for the Tsarevich:	A tsaryevich propyeli
"May his soul rest in heaven."	Vyechnuyu pamyat'.

MEN

Really? It's all a bit confusing.	Vona! chas ot chasu nye lyekhche.
He's living then?	Zhivomu-to?
Why, of course he is, you idiots!	Vot, bezbozhniki-to, pravo!
Dimitry's alive all right!	Zhivomu tsaryevichu!
Just wait, you'll soon find out!	Nu, pogodi uzho!
Boris will live to know it!	Zadast on znat' Borisu.
For they say his troops are not far off.	Uzh pod Kromy, bayut, podoshol.
He comes to claim his rightful throne.	Idyot s polkami na Moskvu.
He'll quickly put to flight	Gromit' po vsyem kontsam
the armies of Boris.	Borisovy polki.
And soon we shall see him upon his	Pobyedny put' vedyot yevo
ancestors' throne, the Tsar whom we long for.	Na otchiy prestol tsaryey pravoslavnykh.
He'll save us all.	Na pomoshch nam,
To death with traitors, and to death with Tsar Boris!	Na smyert' Borisu i Borisovym shchenkam!

OLD MEN

Quiet, quiet, are you crazy?	Shto vy, shto vy, tishe, cherti!
You'll only end up swinging on the gallows!	Al' dybu, da zastyenok pozabyli!

(*They scratch their heads, look round, and start pacing the stage again.*)

Trrr, trrr, trrr, trrr!   Trrr, trrr, trrr, trrr!
Your hat's made of tin, your hat's made of   Zhelyezny kolpak, zhelyezny kolpak!
   tin!
La, la, la, trrr!   Ulyu, lyu, lyu! Trrr!

Enter the Simpleton, in fetters, followed by the urchins. Some of the people drive away the
urchins, who scatter. The Simpleton sits on a stone, mending his bast shoe, and sings, swaying
his body. After a time, the urchins creep around him.

SIMPLETON

Moonlight's shining, and kitten's whining; [39]   Myesyats yedet, kotyonok plachet,
Ivanushka arise,   Yurodivy, vstavay,
Pray to God Almighty.   Bogu promolisya.
Pray to Christ in heaven: Khristu poklonisya.
Christ our Saviour, send us sunlight,   Khristos Bog nash, budyet vyodro,
                    (*absent-mindedly*)
Send us moonlight, send us sunlight . . .   Budyet myesyats, budyet vyodro . . .
Moonlight . . .   Myesyats . . .

URCHINS

Greetings, greetings, good simpleton   Zdravstvuy, zdravstvuy, yurodivy Ivanych!
   Ivanych!
Rise and salute us; show how deeply you   Vstan, nas pochestvuy, v poyas poklonisya
   can bow,   nam,
Then take off your hat. What a heavy hat! Kolpachok to skin! Kolpachok tyazhol!
                   (*They tap his metal hat.*)
Ting, ting, ting. Make it ring!   Dzin, dzin, dzin. Ek zvonit!

SIMPLETON

I found a silver kopek today.   A u menya kopyeyechka yest'.

URCHINS

Nonsense! If you've got one, let us see!   Shutish! Nye naduyesh nas, nye boys!

SIMPLETON
(*He looks for his kopek and then shows it.*)

Look!   Vish!

URCHINS

Whisht!   Fit'!
     (*They snatch the coin from him and run away towards the women.*)

SIMPLETON
(*weeping*)

Ah! ah! ah! Ivanushka's new kopek has   A-a! A! obidyeli Yurodivovo!
   gone!
Ah! ah! Come and give it back to him!   A-a! Otnyali kopyeychku!
Ah! ah! Ah, ah!   A-a! A-a!

     (*The Tsar's procession emerges from the Cathedral. Boyars distribute alms.*)

PEOPLE
(*Women and children on the Cathedral steps, men down stage.*)

Merciful, gracious Tsar, give alms for Our   Kormilets, batyushka, poday Khrista radi!
   Lord's sake.
Kind father, give us alms for Our Lord's   Otyets nash, gosudar, Khrista radi!
   sake.

     (*Boris appears, followed by Shuisky and boyars.*)

PEOPLE

Look, there's the Tsar.   Tsar, Tsar idyot.
                    (*kneeling*)
Tsar, gracious Tsar, give alms for our   Tsar, gosudar, poday Khrista radi!
   Lord's sake!

Merciful Tsar, give alms and bread to your children who starve, for Our Lord's sake!	Kormilyets batyushka, Poshli ty nam milostynku, Khrista radi!

(The women and children follow Boris down stage.)

Mighty Tsar, give us alms, for Our Lord's sake!	Gosudar batyushka, Khrista radi!
Most mighty Tsar, have pity!	Nash batyushka, poday nam!

(kneeling)

Feed us! Feed us! We are starving!	Khlyeba! Khlyeba! Day golodnym!
Feed us! Feed us! Pity your children; give us bread for Our Lord's sake!	Khlyeba, khlyeba, khlyeba poday nam. Batyushka, Khrista radi!

(They bow to the ground.)

SIMPLETON

Ah, ah, ah!	A-a! A-a!

(catching sight of Boris)

Boris, hey Boris!	Boris! a Boris!
Ivanushka's new kopek has gone! Ah, ah, ah!	Obidyeli Yurodivovo! A-a-a!

BORIS
(stopping in front of him)

What makes him cry so?	A chom on plachet?

SIMPLETON

The boys have stolen and run off with it. Command that they be murdered, just as you murdered Dimitry, the young Tsarevich.	Malchishki otnyali kopyeyechku, Veli-ka ikh zaryezat', Kak ty zaryezal malenkovo tsaryevicha.

SHUISKY

Keep quiet, you fool! Seize hold of him at once!	Molchi, durak! Skhvatite duraka!

(A commanding gesture from Boris stops him.)

BORIS

Don't touch him!	Nye tronte!
You holy man, pray for me.	Molis za menya, blazhenny!

(Exit Boris. The Simpleton jumps up. The people, appalled, scatter, still watching the Tsar and his retinue.)

SIMPLETON

No, Boris, I can't, I can't, Boris! I must not pray for a Tsar Herod. The Holy Virgin won't allow it.	Nyet, Boris! nyel'zya, nyel'zya, Boris! Nyel'zya molitsa za tsarya Iroda! Bogodoritsa nye velit.

(He looks round, perplexed; then sits on the stone and resumes his mending.)

Tears are flowing, tears of blood flowing; [39] Weep, weep, O soul; soul of poor Russia. Soon the foe will come and the darkness nears.	Lveytes, lyeytes, slyyozy gorkiye, Plach, plach, dusha pravoslavnaya. Skoro vrag pridyot i nastanyet t'ma,
Shadows hide the light; Dark as darkest night. Sorrow, sorrow on earth; Weep, weep, Russian folk, Poor starving folk!	Tyemen' tyomnaya, Neproglyadnaya. Gore, gore Rusi, Plach, plach, Russky lyud, Golodny lyud!

(He looks round, and then reverts to his mending.)

Curtain.

Act Four

Scene One. *The great reception hall in the Moscow Kremlin. Benches on either side. On the right an entrance door opens on to the main staircase. On the left, an entrance door to the private rooms. Down stage, right, a table covered with scarlet velvet and provided with writing materials. To the left is the Tsar's throne. An emergency sitting of the Council of Boyars is taking place. Shchelkalov, secretary of the Council, enters from the left, a scroll in his hand. He bows to the boyars, who bow in return.* [33]

SHCHELKALOV

Noble boyars met in council!

Sanovityye boyare!

(The boyars rise.)

Our great and mighty lord, Tsar Boris
   Fyodorovich,

Veliky gosudar, tsar Boris Feodorovich,

with due approval of His most exalted
   Holiness

S blagoslovyenyem velikovo svyatyeyshevo
   otsa

the patriarch and father of Russia's church,

I patriarkha vsyeya Rusi,

commands me to proclaim:

Velyel vam obyavit':

(He reads.)

'A scoundrel, thief, and common evil-doer,

'Razboynik, vor, brodyaga bezyzvyestny,

a vagabond and rogue assisted by

Zlodyey i buntovshchikh, vosstavshy
   myatezhom

a disaffected mob of needy hirelings,

S tolpoy nayemnikov golodnykh,

presumes to take the title of Tsarevich,

I imenem tsaryevicha nazavavshis,

and calls himself pretender in succession,

Sebya tsaryom iskonnym velichaya,

supported by the nobles now in banishment,

Soputstvuem boyarami opal'nymi

and by the parasites of Poland.

I vsyakoy svolochyu litovskoy.

He hopes to disenthrone me, your monarch,

Zadumal sokrushit' tron Borisov

and thinks that you, my loyal boyars, will
   support him.

I vas, boyar, k tomu zh nadmyenno
   priglashaet,

(He rolls up the scroll.)

He issues proclamations to that effect.'

O chom zlodyeyskiye ukazy razoslal.'

(The boyars sit down.)

You are summoned to make all haste

Tovo radi, blagoslovyas,

and reach a just and well-considered verdict.

Nad nim pravdivy sud vash sotvorite.

BOYARS
(left) [33]

Come, let's put it to the vote, your lordships.

Shtozh? poydom na golosa, boyare.

BOYARS
(right)

First let us hear from you, your lordships.

Vam pyervym nachinat', boyare.

BOYARS
(left)

Well, our opinion has long been settled.

Da nasche mnyeniye davno gotovo.

(to Shchelkalov)

So write, Andrei Mikhailich,

Pishi, Andrei Mikhaylych.

(rising)

The scoundrel, whoe'er he be, shall die . . .

Zlodyeya, ktob ni byl on, skaznit' . . .

BOYARS
(right)

Wait, your lordships! The man must first be
caught, and then be hanged, so please you.

Stoy, boyare! Vy prezhde izlovi,
A tam skazni, pozhaluy.

BOYARS
(left; sitting down)

Obvious!

Ladno . . .

BOYARS
(right)

No, it is not so obvious.	Nu, nye sovsyem-to ladno.

BOYARS
(left)

Come, come your lordships, don't be foolish!	Da nu, boyare, nye sbivaete ...

(rising)

The scoundrel must instantly be caught, put in chains, and sent for torture. And then be hanged in sight of all the people, and his flesh cast out as carrion.	Zlodyeya, ktob ni byl on, imat' I pytat' na dybye krepko. A tam skaznit' i trup yevo povyesit', Pust' klyuyut vrany golodnyye!

(They bow and sit down.)

BOYARS
(right; rising)

Let his corpse be burnt in public, that all may witness what befell him, and curses be read above his ashes.	Trup yevo predat' sozhzhenyu Na lobnom myestye vsenarodno, I trizhdy proklyast' tot prakh pogeny.

BOYARS
(left)

And his ashes then be scattered and consigned to outer darkness.	I razvyeyat' prakh proklyaty Za zastavami po vyetru.

BOYARS
(all)

So that every trace shall vanish of this evil-hearted traitor.	Shtob i slyed prostyl navyeki Pobrodyagi samozvantsa.

(Some of them rise and go to the table.)

BOYARS
(left; rising)

And everyone who joined in his rebellion shall die.	I kazhdovo, kto s nim yedinomyslit, skaznit'.

BOYARS
(right; rising)

And let their corpses hang in public view.	I trup k pozornomu stolbu pribit'.

BOYARS
(all; rising)

And make this verdict known to all by pronouncement	O chom ukazy razoslat' povsemyestno.
in every country town and every village, yea, read throughout this land in churches great and small,	Po syolam, gorodam i po posadam, Po vysey Rusi chitat' v soborakh i tserkvakh,
in every street and market. And beg Almighty God in humble supplication to pity Holy Russia in her affliction.	Na ploshchadyakh i skhodakh. I gospoda molit' kolenopreklonyonno, Da szhalitsa nad Rusyu mnogostradal'noy.

Deep silence. Enter Shuisky slowly, watching the Boyars.

BOYARS
(aside, in a low voice)

Sad, Shuisky is not with us. Though he's a schemer, how can we ratify our verdict in his absence?	Zhal', Shuyskovo nyet knyazya. Khot' i kramol'nik, A bez nyevo, kazhis, neladno vyshlo mnyenye.

SHUISKY
(bowing)

Forgive me, noble boyars.	Prostite mnye, boyare.

Well, talk of the devil! | Ek, lyogok na pominye ...

SHUISKY

I fear I've kept you somewhat, | Pozapozdal malyenko,
but could not come a single moment | Nye vo vremya pozhalovat' izvolil.
  sooner ...
Affairs of weight and urgency detained my | Dela, zaboty tyazhkiye, lekhko li pravo!
  coming.

BOYARS

Fie, shame on you, Vassil Ivanych; | Stydilsa by, Vasil' Ivanych, v tvoi leta,
how can you deal in treacherous disloyalty | Kramoloyu postydnoy zanimatsa!
  at your age!
The people of our land rebel. | Narod na ploshchadyakh mutit'.
You claim Dimitry is alive ... | Shto zhiv tsaryevich zatveryat! ...

SHUISKY
(startled)

Oh! Really, your lordships! May God | Oy! Shto vy! Boyare! Poboytes Boga!
  forgive you!
How could I, Prince Vassil Ivanych Shuisky, | Mogu li ya vo dni velikoy skorbi,
whose only care is that for Russia's welfare, | V sebye nosya kruchinu Rusi tseloy,
how could I be a traitor to my country? | Mogu li ya kramolam predavatsa?
It's a calumny to say so, and slanderous! | Vsye nagovory zlyye, vse nyedrugi.
(aside)
And for that they hate me! | I za shto nye lyubyat!
(coming closer to the boyars)
Why, even now, in token of the love I bear | Vot i tepyer, lyubya vas vsyey dushoy
  you,
I come to bring you news. | Boyare, khochu predupredit'.
(All the boyars surround him.)
Last night when I had left the royal presence, | Namyedni, ukhodya ot gosudarya,
concerned, and saddened at seeing | Skorbya vsyem syerdtsem,
how distressed the Tsar was, | Radyeya o dushe tsaryovoy,
I found by chance a keyhole and looked in. | Ya v shcholochku sluchayno zaglyanul.
Oh what I saw I scarce can tell you! | O, shto uvidyel ya, boyare!
Haggard, all bathed in sweat and racked | Blyedny, kholodnym potom oblivayas,
  with terror,
his body trembling, | Drozha vsyem tyelom,
he muttered as if mad | Nyesvyazno bormocha
some incoherent words and noises. | Kakiye-to slova chudnyye.
Rolling his eyes bright with frenzy, | Gnyevno ochami sverkaya,
as if some secret torment possessed him, | Kakoy-to mukoy tayno terzayas,
our sovereign lord the Tsar was weeping. | Stradalyets gosudar tomilsa.
Then turning pale, and staring towards a | Vdrug posinyel, glaza ustavil v ugol,
  corner,
he uttered a fearful cry of anguish ... | I strashno stenya i churayas ...

BOYARS

Lies! Lies, Prince! | Lzhosh! Lzhosh, knyaz!

SHUISKY

... recoiling from the ghost of the | ... K tsaryevichu, pogibshemu vzyvaya ...
  Tsarevich ...

BOYARS

What! ... | Shto? ...

SHUISKY

... begged it begone and helplessly repeated: | ... Prizrak yevo bessil'no otgonyaya:
'Go, leave me, child ...' | 'Chur ... chur' sheptal.

Enter Boris, as if trying to drive away a ghost; deeply disturbed, he staggers down stage. [21]

BORIS

Go, go!	Chur, chur!

SHUISKY

Leave me, child!	Chur, ditya!

SHCHELKALOV
(seeing Boris)

Silence! Look . . . the Tsar!	Tishe! Tsar . . . tsar . . .

BOYARS

God above!	Gospodi!

(They step back, watching Boris.)

BORIS

Leave me, child!	Chur, ditya!

BOYARS

O God above, Lord of mercy, protect us!	O, gospodi! S nami krestnaya sila!

BORIS
(coming down to the footlights) [21]

Go . . . go!	Chur, chur!
Who says the child was murdered?	Kto govorit: ubiytsa?
It can't be true!	Ubiytsy nyet!
He lives, I tell you . . .	Zhiv, zhiv malyutka!
But Shuisky has proclaimed this evil slander,	A Shuyskovo za lzhivuyu prisyagu
so he shall hang!	Chertertovat'!

SHUISKY
(appalled, and as if asking a blessing on Boris)

May the Lord have mercy on your soul!	Blagodat' gospodnya nad toboy!

BORIS
(listening)

Ah?	A?

(recovering his senses) [35]

I summoned you, my boyars;	Ya sozval vas, boyare,

(going towards the throne)

I need the wisdom of your counsel.	Na vashu mudrost' polagayus;

(He sits down.)

In times of woe and bitter tribulation	V godinu byed i tyazhkikh ispytaniy,
'tis you, my boyars, who can guide me.	Vy mnye pomoshniki, boyare.

SHUISKY
(coming forward and making a deep obeisance)

Most mighty lord and Tsar,	Veliky gosudar!
permit your most unworthy	Dozvol' mnye, nerazumnomu,
slave and councillor	Smirennomu rabu,
to beg a favour of you . . .	Slovo molvit'.
Here, awaiting at the door,	Zdyes, u Krasnovo kryl'tsa,
Pimen the hermit humbly craves permission	Starets smirenny zhdyot soizvolyenya
to gain admittance to Your Majesty.	Predstat' pred ochi tvoi svyetlyye.
He's virtuous and holy, all know him and revere him;	Muzh pravdy i sovyeta, muzh zhizni bezuprechnoy,
he wishes to disclose some great secret to you.	Velikuyu on taynu povyedat' khochet.

BORIS

So be it: go summon him.	Byt' tak. Zovi yevo!

Exit Shuisky.

| Perhaps his message will bring me consolation | Besyeda startsa, byt' mozhet, uspokoit |
| and calm the suffering of my racked and tortured soul! . . . | Trevogu taynuyu, izmuchennoy dushi! |

Shuisky re-enters, followed by Pimen, who observes the assembly, while standing at the door, stares at Boris intently, and then approaches him. [8]

PIMEN

A humble hermit,	Smirenny inok
who has no thoughts for secular concerns,	V delakh mirskikh nye mudry sudiya,
is bold enough to crave a hearing . . .	Derzaet dnes podat' svoy golos . . .

BORIS
(*perturbed*)

| Speak freely, holy man, all are waiting . . . | Rasskazyvay, starik, vsyo, shto znaesh, |
| tell your story. | Bez utayki. |

PIMEN

My story will be short and simple	Rassakaz moy budyet prost i kratok
and tells the wondrous tidings	Beskhitrostnaya povest'
of Heaven's providence and mercy . . .	O divnom promsylye Gospodnem!
One evening, when all was still,	[34] Odnazhdy, v vecherniy chas,
there came to me a shepherd, already old and wizened,	Prishol ko mnye pastukh, uzhe mastity starets
who told me of a wondrous revelation.	I taynu mnye chudyesnuyu povyedal:
From early childhood, he told me,	'Yeshcho rebyonkom', skazal on,
he was blind and since that time	'Ya oslyep i s toy pory
had not known light from darkness. both seemed alike.	Nye znal ni dnya ni nochi Do starosti.
No remedy could cure him	Naprasno ya lechilsa
in vain he tried all herbs and incantations,	I zeliyem i taynym nasheptanyem,
in vain he bathed his eyes in hope of sight	Naprasno ya iz kladezey svyatykh
with waters brought from holy fountains . . .	Kropil vodoy tselyebnoy ochi . . .
all vainly!	Naprasno!
And thus he grew so used to dark,	I tak ya k t'me svoyey privyk,
that in his dreams at night the sights	Shto dazhe sny moi
he once had known	Mnye vidyennykh veshchey
appeared no longer;	Uzh nye yavlyalis,
his dreaming was but hearing . . .	A snilis tol'ko zvuki.
Once, while deep in sleep, a voice spoke . . .	Raz v glubokom snye, vdrug slyshu
yes, a child's voice called out to him,	Dyetsky golos zovyot menya,
how clearly it called:	Tak vnyatno zovyot:

(*Boris shudders, listens in deep perturbation, and grows more and more restless.*)

'Rise, grandfather, rise,	'Vstan, dyedushka, vstan,
and go to Uglich town	Idi ty v Uglichgrad,
and enter there the great Cathedral,	Zaydi v sobor Probrazhenya,

(*Boris rises in his seat and wipes his brow.*)

kneel down and pray beside my little tombstone.	Tam pomolis ty nad moyey mogilkoy.
For, grandfather, I am Dimitry, Tsarevich; [9]	Znay, dyedushka: Dimitriy ya, tsaryevich,
The Lord has chosen me to dwell among his angels	Gospod' priyal menya v lik angelov svoikh
and henceforth to work great miracles for Russia' . . .	I ya tepyer Rusi veliky chudo-tvorets' . . .

(*Boris sinks back onto his throne.*)

He roused himself . . . and pondered . . .	Prosnulsa ya . . . podumal . . .
then he called his grandson	Vzyal s soboyu vnuka
and started on the journey.	I v dal'niy put' poplyolsa.
And scarcely had he knelt beside the tombstone,	I tol'ko shto sklonilsa nad mogilkoy,

(Boris, in deepest agitation, listens intently.)

when he was healed of blindness,	Tak khorosho vdrug stalo
his eyes were filled with tears,	I slyozy polilis,
with silent, freely flowing tears,	Obil'no, tikho polilis
for all was clear now: he saw the light	I ya uvidyel i Bozhy svyet,
his grandson and the grave . . .	I vnuka, i mogilky'.

Boris, with a great cry, clutches his heart. The boyars run to his assistance. Exit Pimen quickly. [21]

BORIS

Ah! Help me! Help me! I'm stifling!	Oy; dushno! dushno! svyetu!

(He falls, swooning, held in the arms of the boyars. They talk in whispers. Some rush out for help. General confusion. Boris recovers.)

My son must come at once!	Tsaryevicha skorey!
Oh! Death is near: shroud me!	Okh, tyazhko mnye! Skhimu!

(The boyars sit Boris in a chair. Shuisky hurries out to fetch the Tsarevich; others, to fetch the Patriarch at the Chudov Monastery. Only five of them remain around Boris. Fyodor rushes in and falls into his father's arms, who embraces him.) [18]

Now leave us here, let all withdraw!	Ostavte nas! uydite vsye!

(Exeunt all but Boris and Fyodor.)

Farewell, my son, I am dying . . . [35]	Proshchay, moy syn, umirayu.
This day you'll reign here in my place.	Seychas ty tsarstvovat' nachnyosh.
Don't ask of me by what dark path	Nye sprashivay, kakim putyom
I came to Russia's throne . . .	Ya tsarstvo priobryol . . .
that's past . . . you need not know.	Tebye nye nuzhno znat'.

(solemnly)

You'll reign henceforth as lawful ruler,	Ty tsarstvovat' po pravu budyesh,
you are my first-born,	Kak moy naslyednik,
my son, and true successor.	Kak syn moy pervorodny.
Fyodor! My well-beloved Tsarevich! [18]	Syn moy! Ditya moyo rodnoye!
Our kingdom is in danger;	Venyets tebye dostalsa
see that you defend it.	V tyazhkuyu godinu,
Beware! Fear the pretender!	Silyon zloy samozvanyets!
The name he took strikes terror in my heart.	On imenem uzhasnym opolchon.
You must contend with treacherous subjects,	Vokrug tebya boyar kramola,
rebellious armies . . .	Izmyena voyska,
famine, plague . . .	Glad i mor.

(clutching his heart)

Listen, Fyodor!	Slushay, Fyodor:
Put no trust in the cunning advice of boyars;	Nye vyeryaysa navyetam boyar kramol'nykh;
keep careful watch upon their secret conspiracies with Poland;	Zorko sledi za ikh snoshenyami taynymi s Litvoyu.
condemn hateful treason severely, be merciless and strong;	Izmyenu karay bez poshchady, bez milosti karay.
study the thoughts of your people, use their simple wisdom.	Strogo vnikay v sud narodny, sud nelitsemyerny.
Be the guardian and prop of Russia's holy faith;	Stoy na strazhe bortsom za vyeru pravuyu,
hold in awe God's blessed saints and his angels;	Svyato chti svyatykh ugodnikov Bozhikh.

(warmly)

Keep your conscience pure and innocent, Fyodor;	Soblyudi ty chistotu svoyu, Feodor;
the strength it gives will guide you and carry you onward to salvation.	V nyey moshch tvoya i sila, I razuma krepost', i spasenye.

(placing his hand on his heart)

Protect your gentle sister, guard her well, my son; [17]	Sestru svoyu, tsaryevnu, sberegi, moy syn,
she has but you to give her help and guidance,	Ty yey, odin khran:tel' ostayoshsa,
dearest Xenia, our cherished angel.	Nashey Ksenii, golubke chistoy.

102

(very solemnly, in rapt prayer, his voice gradually weakening; almost spoken)

God above, God above, behold, I pray,	Gospodi! Gospodi! Vozzri, molyu,
a sinful father's humble tears!	Na slyozy greshnovo ottsa!
I pray not selfishly,	Nye za sebya molyu,
not for myself, O Father!	Nye za seby, moy Bozhe!

(placing both his hands on Fyodor's head)

Saviour, Lord of mercy, from on high	S gorney nepristupnoy vysoty
send down Thy saving grace and love	Prolyev ty blagodatny svyet
on those innocents, my children,	Na chad moikh nevinnykh ...
young and helpless ...	Krotkikh, chistykh ...
Angels and Cherubim!	Sily nebyesnyye!
You who guard o'er the Deity ...	Strazhi trona predvyechnovo

(embracing his son as if to protect him)

I pray you, spread your wings to shield my children;	Krylami svyetlymi vy okhranite
protect my son and daughter from harm and sin	Moyo ditya rodnoye ot byed i zol,
and from temptation ...	ot iskusheniy.

(He draws Fyodor close to him and kisses him. Off-stage, a bell slowly tolls the death knell. [5a] Boris listens.)

Hark! It's the knell of death!	Zvon! Pogrebal'ny zvon!

CHOIR
(off-stage)

Weep ye, weep ye, sons of men,	Plachte, plachte, lyudiye.
for his course is run ...	Nyest'bo zhizni v nyom ...

BORIS

The funeral dirge! Clothe me ...	Nadgrobny vopl'! Skhima,
a robe of sackcloth ...	Svyataya skhima,
as monk I meet my end ...	v monakhi tsar idyot.

CHOIR

His eyes are for ever closed,	I nyemy usta yevo
and his lips are silent!	I nye dast otvyeta
Weep ye! Alleluia!	Plachte! Alliluya!

FYODOR
(in tears)

O my lord, take comfort	Gosudar, uspokoysya!
for God will help us!	Gospod' promoshet.

BORIS

No, no, Fyodor: death's knell has struck ...	Nyet, nyet, syn moy, chas moy probil ...

CHOIR
(drawing nearer)

I see a little child who breathes his last ...	Vizhu mladyentsa umirayushcha ...

BORIS

Mercy! Mercy! Mercy, Lord!	Bozhe! Bozhe! Tyazkho mnye!
With prayer I'll expiate my sin!	Uzhel' grekha ne zamolyu?

CHOIR

I stand weeping, I mourn;	I rydayu, plachu;
he struggles, he writhes and sobs.	Myatyotsa, trepyeshchet on, ...

BORIS

Oh, cruel death, your agony torments me!	O, zlaya smyert'! kak muchisch ty zhestoko!

CHOIR

In vain imploring, praying:	...i k pomoshchi vzyvaet,
but there is no salvation ...	I nyet yemu spasyenya.

(The boyars and choir of monks enter by the main door. Boris rises, they stand still.)

BORIS

Await my orders . . . your Tsar commands!	Povremenite . . . ya tsar yeshcho!
(He clutches his heart and falls into his seat.)	
Your Tsar commands . . . Mercy! Death!	Ya tsar yeshcho! Bozhe! Smyert'!
(spoken very weakly)	
Forgive me, Lord!	Prosti menya!
(to the Boyars, and pointing to his son)	
There, there's your Tsar . . . Tsar . . .	Vot! Vot tsar vash . . . tsar . . .
Forgive me . . .	Prostite . . .
(in a whisper)	
Forgive me . . .	Prostite . . .

Boris collapses and dies. Deep silence. The boyars stand as if stunned, heads down, hands crossed, struck motionless by the Tsar's last words. [19]

BOYARS
(in a whisper)

Amen.	Uspnye!

The curtain falls very slowly.

Scene Two. *A clearing in a forest near Kromy. To the right a slope with the town walls visible in the distance beyond it. From the slope, a roadway crosses the stage. Ahead there is a forest thicket. By the road is a big tree-stump. It is night. When the curtain rises, the cries of a crowd of vagabonds are heard off stage. The crowd of vagabonds rushes down the slope* [36] *. Among them is the boyar Khrushchov, bound, bareheaded and his fine coat torn.*

CROWD

Let's put him here,	Vali syuda!
and sit him on this log a moment . . .	Na pyen sadim na pyen, rebyata!
(They sit Khrushchov on a log.)	
. . . like that!	Vot tak!
And as he may cry out	A shtob nye bol 'no vyl,
and hurt his noble throat with too much shouting,	Shtob gorla-to boyarskovo nye portil . . .
give him a gag!	Zakonopat'.
(They gag him with a piece of his coat, which they tie with his belt.)	
That's it! Wait, fellows,	Vazhno! Shtozh, bratsy?
we can't leave him lonely, let's mount a guard of honour!	Al' tak, bez pochotu boyarina ostavim?
Yes, he deserves it! He shall have it!	Tak, bez pochot! Tak nye ladno!
Never forget that he's a boyar!	Vsyozh on Borisov voyevoda.
(Some of them begin to build a fire.)	
He's a boyar to a Tsar who stole the throne he sits on,	Boris-ot vorovski prestolom tsarskim pravit,
but he has robbed the royal thief!	A on u vora voroval!
Good, then let us do him honour	Shtozh? Za to yemu pochot,
as a prince of thieves!	Kak voru dobromu!
Hey! You there, Fomka! Epikhan!	Ey! Ryndy! Fomka! Yepikhan!
Come and stand by him! That's right!	Za boyarina! Vazhno!
(Two men, armed with cudgels, take their stand behind Khrushchov.)	
Something is missing still:	Shtoyto za nyevidal'!
so fine a lord is never	Al' nikoli boyarin nash
to be seen without a sweetheart!	Zasnobushki nye vyedal?
That's quite unheard of!	Kudy tye k chortu!
A lord without a sweetheart	Boyarin bez zaznoby,
is a pie that is empty and only crust!	Shto pirog bez nachinki, odin sukhar!
Afimya! Afimya!	Afimya! golubka!
The gossips tell us	Tebye uzh, bayut,
that you've already passed a hundred.	Vtoraya sotnya podstupila.
If that's so you're safe enough!	Tak ono nye opazno.
So come and kiss the boyar lovingly!	Vali, krasavitsa, k boyarinu!
Come on!	Vali!

(From the crowd an old woman, moaning and coughing, comes towards Khrushchov. The crowd bursts out laughing.)

Ha, ha, ha!	Kha, kha, kha!

Bravo! Let's praise the loving pair!	Ladno. Davayte velichat'!
Hey, women, you begin!	Ey, baby, zavodi!
Come on, women, you begin!	Ey, vy baby, zavodi!

(*They form a half-circle round Krushchov.*)

Like a falcon that's chained in captivity, [37]	Nye sokol letit po podnebyesyu,
Like a stallion robbed of its liberty,	Nye borzy kon mchitsa po polyu.
Silent here sits our noble boyar,	Sidnem sisit boyarinushka
Lost in deepest thought.	Dumu dumayet.
Honour the great boyar, [38]	Slava boyarinu!
Slave of our wicked Tsar.	Slava Borisovu!
Hail him!	Slava!

(*They bow.*)

Wait, women, our nobleman has come without a cudgel.	Stoy, baby! Dubinki u boyarina nye vidno.
Can't spare a cudgel, let this whip do!	Chevo dubinki? Sunte plyotku.

(*They force a whip into his hand.*)

Like that. On with the song!	Vot tak. Dal'she valvay.
Silent he sits as he's wondering [37]	Sidnem sidit, dumu dumaet,
How he can please Tsar Boris again;	Kak by Borisu v ugodushku,
How he'll win the tyrant's favour,	Kak vy voru na pomoch
Flogging to death honest folk!	Zabit, zaporot' lyud chestnoy.
Honour the great boyar, [38]	Slava boyarinu,
Slave of our wicked Tsar!	Slava Borisovu!
Hail him!	Slava!

(*They come closer to him and bow.*)

We shall not forget all that we owe to you, [37]	Chestyu, pochestyu ty nas povazhival,
How you made us bear hardship and servitude;	V buryu, nyepogod', da v bezdorozhiye,
Blown by storms and beaten with whips,	Na rebyatakh nashykh pokatyval,
We work day and night as our children starve!	Tonkoy plyotkoy postyogival.
Honour the great boyar, [38]	Slava boyarinu!
Slave of our wicked Tsar!	Slava Borisovu!
Praise him and honour his name for ever!	Okh, uzh i slava-zh tebye, boyarin
Praise him! Honour him!	Slava vyechnaya!

They bow to the ground. / The following incident is usually omitted if the 'St Basil scene' is performed. / A Simpleton runs in from the left along the roadway; he is hung with chains, barefoot, wears an iron hat, and holds a bast-shoe in his hand. He is pursued by a crowd of urchins who have driven him out of the thicket.

URCHINS

Trrr, trrr, trrr, trrr!	Trrr, trrr, trrr, trrr!
Your hat's made of tin, your hat's made of tin!	Zhelyezny kolpak, zhelyezny kolpak!
La, la, la, trrr!	Ulyu, lyu, lyu, trrr!

(*Some of the crowd shake their fists at the urchins, who run off to the side. The Simpleton sits on a stone and sings, swaying his body and mending his bast-shoe.*)

SIMPLETON

Moonlight's shining and kitten's whining; [39]	Myesyats yedet, kotyonok plachet,
Ivanushka arise,	Yurodivy, vstavay,
Pray to God Almighty.	Bogu promoisya,
Pray to Christ in heaven;	Khristu poklonisya
Christ our Saviour, send us sunlight,	Kristos Bog nash, budyet vyodro,

(*absent-mindedly*)

Send us moonlight, send us sunlight ...	Budyet myesyats, budyet vyodro ...
Moonlight ...	Myesyats ...

URCHINS

Greetings, greetings, good simpleton Ivanych!	Zdravstvuy, zdravstvuy, yurodivy Ivanych!
Rise and salute us; show how deeply you can bow,	Vstan, nas pochestvuy, v poyas poklonisya nam,
Then take off your hat. What a heavy hat!	Kolpachok to skin! Kolpachok tyazhol!

(They tap his metal hat.)

Ting, ting, ting. Make it ring!	Dzin, dzin, dzin. Ek zvonit?!

SIMPLETON

I found a silver kopek today.	A u menya kopyeyechka yest'.

URCHINS

Nonsense! If you've got one, let us see!	Shutish! Nye naduyesh nas, nye boys!

SIMPLETON
(looking for his kopek and showing it)

Look!	Vish!

URCHINS
(snatching the coin from him and running away towards the women)

Wisht!	Fit'!

SIMPLETON
(weeping)

Ah! ah! ah! Ivanushka's new kopek has gone!	A-a! A! Obideli yurodivovo!
Ah! ah! Come and give it back to him! Ah! Ah! Ah!	A-a! Otnyali kopyyeyechku! A-a! A-a! A-a!

(He settles down against a stone and pretends to sleep.)

MISSAIL AND VARLAAM
(approaching off-stage right) [40]

Darkness has swallowed sun and moon,	Solntse, luna pomyerknuli,
Stars leave their course in the skies above,	Zvyozdy s nebyes pokatilisya,
The day of judgement now is near at hand	Vselyennaya voskolebalasya,
To purge the sinfulness of Tsar Boris.	Ot tyazhkovo grekha Borisova
Monsters and dragons prowl through the land,	Brodit zveryo nevidannoye,
Foul beasts and serpents ravage the land,	Rodit zveryo neslykhannoye,
And they feed on the flesh of the victims they kill	Pozhiraet tela chelovyecheskiye
Because of the sins of Tsar Boris.	Vo slavu grekha Borisova.

MISSAIL
(nearer)

God-fearing folk live in misery,	Muchat, putayut bozhy lyud,

CROWD
(listening, and moving towards the right)

Who can these be?	Shto b to bylo?

MISSAIL

Oppressed and starved by their wicked Tsar,	A muchat slugi Borisovy,

CROWD

Holy fathers come to us from Moscow ...	Ot Moskvy idut svyatyye startsy,
What will they say?	Shto b to bylo?

VARLAAM

For the powers of evil work in him ...	Naushchenyem sily adovoy,

CROWD

Come to proclaim the guilt of Boris and the hunger and torture	Pyesnyu vedut o koznyakh Borisa, O pytkakh sviryepykh, o mukakh zhestokikh,
that Christian people must suffer.	Shto tyerpit lyud nepovinny.

VARLAAM AND MISSAIL

To further the kingdom of Beelzebub.	Vo slavu prestola sataninskovo.

(They enter.)

Russia is groaning and bleeds to death,	Stonet, myatyotsa svyataya Rus,
She struggles in the clutches of an infidel,	A stonet pod rukoy bogootstupnika,
A regicide who murdered the Tsarevich	Pod proklyatoy rukoy tsareubiytsy,
For the glory and triumph of iniquity!	V proslavlyenye grekha nezamolimovo!

CROWD

Hurrah!	Gayda!
Casting off our chains of bondage,	[41] Raskhodilas, razgulyalas
we shall set our people free . . .	Udal' molodyetskaya.
Thirst for vengeance has	Pyshet polymem
stirred our youthful blood.	Krov Kazatskaya.
Valiant Russian people,	Podnimalas so dna,
end your life of need, show your might!	Sila pododonnaya.
You must fight for liberty	Podnimalas, teshilas
and put the foe to flight!	Neugomonnaya!
Hey!	Goy!

(women)

We shall vanquish tyranny,	Oy, ty sila, silushka,
we shall end all our misery!	Oy, ty sila bedovaya!
Show your strength, O warriors,	Ty nye vyday molodtsev,
lead us on to victory! Hey! Hey!	Molodtsev udalyikh! Goy! Goy!

(men)

Cossack valour revives in us,	Oy, ty sila bedovaya!
we'll be victorious!	Oy, ty sila groznaya,
We shall vanquish all tyranny,	Oy, nye vyday ty molodtsev,
we shall end all our misery!	Oy, nye vyday udalyikh!

(all)

Our strength rises, it burns in us!	Oy, silushka bedovaya!
For hatred makes us pitiless,	Ty day im ponatyeshitsa,
and rouses us to victory!	Ty day im ponasytitsa!

VARLAAM, OLDER VAGABONDS

Russian people sing for joy,	Vosprimite, lyudiye,
and greet your lawful Tsar!	tsarya zakonnovo!

MISSAIL, YOUNGER VAGABONDS

Greet your Tsar whom God has preserved from death,	Vosprimite Bogom spasyonnovo,
greet your lawful Tsar whom the Lord has saved.	Ot ubiytsy Bogom ukrytovo.

MISSAIL, VARLAAM, CROWD

Sing for joy, and loudly acclaim your Tsar, Dimitry, the son of Ivan!	Vosprimite, lyudiye, tsarya Dimitriya Ivanovicha!

CROWD

Tsar Boris has ordered his servants	Ryshchut, brodyat slugi Borisa
to torture innocent people . . .	Pytayut lyud nepovinny . . .
Tsar Boris and those who surround him	Ryshchut, brodyat slugi Borisa
torture innocent people . . .	Muchat lyud nepovinny . . .
Starve and oppress us, torture and kill us.	Pytkoy pytayut, dushat v zastyenkye,
They never show any mercy.	Izbyt' khotyat pravoslavnykh,
Torture and murder innocent people!	Muchat, pytayut, dushat v zastyenkye,
Torture and murder innocent people!	Lyud nepovinny, lyud nepovinny.
Death! Death to him! Death to Boris!	Smyert'! Smyert' yemu! Smyert' Borisu!
Death to those who murder!	Smyert'! tsareubiytse!
Death to Boris! We'll put the Tsar to death!	Smyert' Borisu! Tsareubiytse smyert'!

LAVITSKY, CHERNIKOVSKY
(off-stage)

Domine, Domine, salvum fac Regem,	Domine, Domine, salvum fac Regem,
Regem Demetrium Moscoviae,	Regem Demetrium Moscoviae,

Salvum fac, salvum fac
Regem Demetrium omnis Russiae,
Salvum fac, salvum fac Regem Demetrium.

Salvum fac, salvum fac
Regem Demetrium omnis Russiae,
Salvum fac, salvum fac Regem Demetrium.

CROWD

Who's coming now? What travellers are these?
What a row they're making!
Cursed parasites!

Kovo yeshcho nelyokhkaya nesyot?

Slovno volki voyut!
Shto za dyavoly?

(Part of the crowd rushes left towards the Jesuits.)

LAVITSKY, CHERNIKOVSKY
(nearer)

Domine, Domine, salvum fac
Regem Demetrium salvum fac.

Domine, Domine, salvum fac
Regem Demetrium salvum fac.

VARLAAM
(to Missail)

Devil take these Jesuits!
They come to welcome the Tsarevich as we have done.
We shan't let them, my good Missail!

Voronyo poganoye!
Podi-ka, tozhe vozglashayut tsaryevicha!
Nye popustim, otyets Misail

MISSAIL, VARLAAM

We shan't let them!

Nye popustim!

LAVITSKY, CHERNIKOVSKY
(entering)

Domine, Domine salvum fac
Regem Demetrium Moscoviae.

Domine, Domine salvum fac
Regem Demetrium Moscoviae.

MISSAIL, VARLAAM
(to the crowd, shouting)

Let's hang the cursed ravens!

Dushi voron prokyatykh!

CROWD

Hurrah! To death! To death!
Blood-sucking vampires!
Evil-scheming sorcerers!

Gayda! Dushi! Davi!
A, krovososy,
Kolduny poganyye!

(They seize the Jesuits.)

VARLAAM

Let us exalt them and hang them nearer heaven!

Da voznesutsa na drevo blagolyepno.

MISSAIL, VARLAAM

And they will sing quite another tune as they dangle there!

Da vosproslavyat vsyelyenuyu glasom veliim.

CROWD

Hurrah!

Gayda!

(They pinion the Jesuits.)

LAVITSKY, CHERNIKOVSKY

Sanctissima Virgo juva, juva . . .

Sanctissima Virgo juva, juva . . .

VARLAAM
(to the crowd)

Tight as you can!

Krepche vyazhi!

LAVITSKY, CHERNIKOVSKY

. . . servos tuos!

. . . servos tuos!

VARLAAM

And bind their hands to stop them escaping!

Da presechotsa maniye dlanyey,

Hurrah!   Gayda!

LAVITSKY, CHERNIKOVSKY

Sanctissima Virgo juva, juva . . .   Sanctissima Virgo juva, juva . . .

VARLAAM

For their end has come, nothing can save   Da otrinyetsa pomoshch desnitsy!
  them!

LAVITSKY, CHERNIKOVSKY

  . . . servos tuos! Sanctissima . . .   . . . servos tuos! Sanctissima . . .

CROWD

Come on, let us hang them!   Gayda! Na osinu!
            (They drag the Jesuits into the forest.)

LAVITSKY, CHERNIKOVSKY

Virgo juva servos tuos, servos tuos . . . Virgo juva servos tuos, servos tuos . . .

*The Simpleton stands up, looks round, and lies down again. The Pretender's trumpet-call
sounds from the forest. Enter horsemen in white capes, and foot-soldiers bearing torches.*

MISSAIL, VARLAAM

Hail to our Tsar most glorious,   Slava tebye, tsaryevichu,
whom God has saved for us!   Bogom spasyonnomu.
Hail to our Tsar most glorious,   Slava tebye, tsaryevichu,
through God restored to us!   Bogom ukrytomu!

CROWD
(off-stage)

Hail Tsar most glorious,   Slava tsaryevichu,
whom God has saved for us!   Bogom spasyonnomu,
God chose thee, God saved thee!   Bogom ukrytomu!
Hail to our Tsar,   Slava tebye,
through God restored to us!   Bogom spasyonnomu!

            (The crowd and the Jesuits surge back on stage.)

CROWD

Long live our sovereign, Dimitry Ivanovich! Zhivi i zdravstvuy, Dimitry Ivanovich!
Glory, glory, glory!   Slava! Slava! Slava!

*The Pretender, wearing a white cape, plumed helmet and a cuirass, rides in on horseback.
Soldiers in white capes hold his horse by the bridle.*

PRETENDER
(from his horse, to the crowd) [9]

We, Dimitry Ivanovich,   My, Dimitry Ivanovich,
by the will of God above   Bozhyim izvolyeniyem
Tsarevich of all the Russias,   Tsaryevich vseya Rusii,
heir to the throne by royal lineage,   Knyaz ot kolyena predkov nashikh,
call on you, the tyrant's victims,   Vas, gonimykh Godunovym
to follow us, and hereby promise   Zovyom k sebye i obeshchaem
mercy and protection.   Milost' i zashchitu.

KHRUSHCHOV
(Watched by the crowd, he shakes off his bonds.)

God above! Son of Ivan, all glory to thee!   Gospodi! Syn Ioannov, slava tebye!
            (He bows to the ground.)

PRETENDER
(to Khrushchov)

Rise, good boyar!   Vstan, boyarin!
            (to the crowd)

Now forwards, take up arms;   Za nami, v slavny boy!
defend your sacred country!   Na rodinu svyatuyu!

| March on! Moscow awaits us! | V Moskvu, v kreml' zlatovyerkhy! |

*Exit the Pretender, via the slope, right. Off-stage, the heavy tolling of an alarm bell is heard.
All except the Simpleton follow the Pretender.*

CROWD

| Glory to thee, Tsar of this land! | Slava tebye, Dimitriy Ivanovich! |

LAVITSKY, CHERNIKOVSKY

Deo gloria, gloria!	Deo gloria, gloria!
	(off-stage)
Deo gloria, gloria!	Deo gloria, gloria!

CROWD
(off-stage)

| Glory to thee Dimitry Ivanovich! | Slava tebye, Dimitriy Ivanovich! |

*The Simpleton starts up, looks round, then sits down on the stone and sings, swaying his body.
From off-stage right, the sound of a tocsin and the glow of a great fire. The crowd is shouting.*

SIMPLETON [39]

Tears are flowing, tears of blood flowing;	Lyeytes, lyeytes, slyozy gorkiye,
Weep, weep, O soul; soul of poor Russia.	Plach, plach, dusha pravolsavnaya.
Soon the foe will come and the darkness nears.	Skoro vrag pridyot i nastanyet t'ma.
Shadows hide the light;	Tyemen tyomnaya,
Dark as darkest night.	Neproglyadnaya.
Sorrow, sorrow on earth;	Gore, gore Rusi;
Weep, weep, Russian folk,	Plach, plach Russky lyud,
Poor starving folk!	Golodny lyud!

The deep sounds of the tocsin continue to be heard off-stage. He shudders, watching the glow.

Final Curtain.

Boris Christoff in the title role at Covent Garden. (photo: Donald Southern; Covent Garden Archives)

Discography Available recordings in stereo (unless asterisked *) and in Russian. Cassette tape numbers are also given. An exceptionally interesting review of all performances on record by David Hamilton is contained in *Opera on Record* (ed. Alan Blyth, Hutchinson 1979).

Conductor Company/Orchestra	*Dobrowen* **French National Radio**	*Karajan* **Vienna PO**	*Melik-Pashaev* **Bolshoi**	*ORIGINAL VERSION* *Semkow* **Polish Radio Orchestra**
Boris	Christoff	Ghiaurov	London	Talvela
Shuisky	Bielecki	Maslennikov	Shulpin	Paprocki
Dimitry	Gedda	Spiess	Ivanovsky	Gedda
Marina	Zareska	Vishnevskaya	Arkhipova	Kinasz
Varlaam	Christoff	Diakov	Gueleva	Haugland
Missail		Paunov	Zahjarov	Pustelak
Rangoni		Kelemen	Kibkalo	Hiolski
Pimen	Christoff	Talvela	Reshetin	Mroz
Disc number UK	SLS5072 *	SET514–7	77396	SLS1000
Disc number USA	ID6101 *	OSA1439	D4S–696	SX–3844
Tape number		K81K43		TC–SLS1000
Excerpts		SET557		4X4X–3844

Excerpts

	Artists	Number
Excerpts	Nesterenko, Bolshoi Company, cond. Simonov	ASD4006
Excerpts	Rossi-Lemeni, San Francisco SO, Stokowski	DA9002
Excerpts	Soloists, Sofia PO, Raychev	HMB 130
Boris's monologue	Ghiaurov	SXL 6859
Death of Boris	Kipnis	RL 30439
Orchestral Medley (arr. Stokowski)	Suisse Romande, Stokowski	SDD 456

Bibliography

Mussorgsky's biographer in English is M.D. Calvocoressi (*Modest Mussorgsky: his Life and Works*, London 1956, revised 1967). The short biography in the Master Musician series, also written by Calvocoressi, was completed and revised by Gerald Abraham (Dent, 1974).

Specific studies of *Boris Godunov* by Abraham are contained in *Slavonic and Romantic Music* (London, 1968) and by R.W. Oldani in 19th Century Music, ii (1978–9) ('*Boris Godunov* and the Censor').

The Mussorgsky Reader: a Life of M.P. Mussorgsky in Letters and Documents (edited by J. Leyda and S. Bertensson, New York, 1947, revised 1970) is a very valuable anthology of the correspondence and reminiscences of the composer's highly articulate contemporaries.

A Cambridge Opera handbook on the opera, edited by Geoffrey Norris, is currently in preparation.

Pushkin's play is not readily available in translation.

David Lloyd-Jones's edition of the score, with notes, is published by Oxford

3907